Vertical Lines III

A Compilation of Sarcasm, Word Play, and Witticisms

Edited By

ANDREW A. FELDER

Published by CREST Publications Group, Fort Worth, TX

ISBNs

9798885266413 (Print)
9798885266406 (E-book)

www.crestpublicationsgroup.com

COVER DESIGN: SHUMAILA REHMAN
TECHNICAL DIRECTOR: MARIA TARIQ

When I was a young boy, I noticed in *MAD Magazine* that the gutters separating the two pages often contained humorous phrases. One in particular stuck with me these many years - "If Tuesday Weld married Frederick March III, she'd be Tuesday, March the Third." I thought that was so funny that I laughed out loud, even though I was alone at the time. I also resolved right then that if I ever published a magazine, I was going to do that, too – put funny or meaningful lines in the gutters of many of the pages.

Fast forward 100 years (or so it feels like) and I do publish a magazine – the network – and I have been putting these short one-liners (sometimes there are actually two lines) in the gutters of the magazine's pages for over a decade. We call them Vertical Lines.

They come from anywhere and everywhere – words of wisdom, insults, funny quotes, word play – just fun and interesting stuff. It was one of our readers who (while submitting a few lines for us to use in the network) suggested compiling them into a book – and "Viola!" [the immortal word of Kelly Bundy on the television sitcom *Married With Children*], there it was! And here it is – timeless!

And now, years later, this is Book III. And, as long as you keep enjoying them, we'll keep them coming. We hope you enjoy them! And if you do, go to www.crestnetwork.com and see new ones in every issue of the network. (There's more humor there, too.) 😀

My mind is still as sharp as a tack. That's why they call me 'Tacky.'

"Last week, I stated this woman was the ugliest woman I had ever seen. I have since been visited by her sister, and now wish to withdraw that statement." (Mark Twain)

If I had a dollar for every time I left something unfinished,

"Everyone said to Vincent van Gogh, 'You can't be a great painter, you only have one ear. And you know what he said? 'I can't hear you.'" (Steve Carell)

If I woke up and nothing hurt, I would think I was dead.

My friend David lost his ID. Now we just call him 'Dav.'

I got fired from my job because I asked customers whether they would prefer 'smoking' or 'non—smoking.' I've since learned that the preferred terms are 'cremation' and 'burial.'

"Be careful about reading health books. You may die of a misprint."
(Mark Twain)

I asked my childhood sweetheart, my best friend, and the love of my life, to marry me. All three said no.

15 + 15 is thirty and 16 + 16 is thirty, too.

My husband and I decided we don't want to have children. We will be telling them tonight.

"By the time a man is wise enough to watch his step, he's too old to go anywhere." (Billy Crystal)

My husband texted me after an argument to say that I had been very condescending. To be totally honest, I was surprised he could spell it.

I used to live on a houseboat, and I started dating the girl next door. It didn't work out, though. We just drifted apart.

What has four letters, occasionally has twelve letters, always has six letters, but never has five letters?

My girlfriend told me that obesity is in her genes. I told her that that can't be true because she looks fat in her skirt also.

"Don't worry about avoiding temptation. As you grow older, it will avoid you." (Winston Churchill)

At what age is it appropriate for me to tell my dog that he's adopted?

My wife makes me eat candies after I tell jokes. They're my punish mints.

The best place to weigh whales is at a whale weigh station.

"Maybe it's true that life begins at fifty, but everything else starts to wear out, fall out, or spread out." (Phyllis Diller)

My parents sent me to a child psychologist. That kid was no help at all.

Do you know why British people say bri ish? Because they drank the tea.

I recently called an old engineering buddy of mine and asked what he was working on. He replied that he was working on 'aqua thermal treatment of ceramics and aluminum under a constrained environment.' I was impressed until, upon further inquiry, I learned that he was washing dishes with hot water under his wife's supervision.

"By all means, marry. If you get a good wife, you'll become happy; if you get a bad one, you'll become a philosopher." (Socrates)

Aoccdrnig to a rscheearch at Cmabrigde Umnervtisv. it deosnet mttaer in waht oredr the ltteers in wrod are, the olny ipromotnt thing is taht the frist and lsat ltteer be in the rghit pclae. The rest can be a toatl mses and you can sill raed it wouthit porbelm. Tihs is bcuseae the huamn mnid deos not raed ervev letter by istlef, but the word as a wlohe.

A good slogan for the World Health Organization would be WHO Cares.

A priest was checking into a hotel. He asked the clerk: 'I presume that the pornography channel is disabled?' 'No,' replied the clerk; 'it's just regular porn, you pervert!'

I tried sniffing coke once, but the ice cubes got stuck up my nose.

'Audio' is Latin for 'I hear' and 'Video' is Latin for 'I see.'

Dad: 'Hey, Son, what are you drinking?'
Son: 'Soy milk.'
Dad: 'Hola, milk. Soy padre.'

Q: What do you call an indecisive B?
A may—be.

The word 'queue' is just a 'Q' followed by four silent letters.

Your fingers have fingertips, but your toes don't have toetips. Yet, you can tiptoe but not tipfinger.

The ability to speak several languages is a great asset, but the ability to keep your mouth shut in any language is priceless.

She: 'Every time I get in the shower, I think of you.' He: 'Is that because you wish I were there with you?'
She: 'No. It's because the French word for shower is douche.'

If you buy a bigger bed, you'll have more bed but less bedroom.

"Money can't buy you happiness .... but it does bring you a more pleasant form of misery." (Spike Milligan)

Nostalgia isn't what it used to be.

If I had 50 cents for every math exam I failed, I 'd have $6.75.

In college I dated a philosophy major, but she never really knew if I existed or not.

Someone stole the toilet seat at the police station, and they have nothing to go on.

Justice is a dish best served cold. If it were served warm, it would be justwater.

Q: What's the opposite of a croissant?
A: A happy uncle.

Chickens are the only animals you eat before they're born and after they're dead.

Today I learned that human beings eat more bananas than monkeys. I can't remember the last time ate a monkey.

When my uncle died, he wanted his remains pressed into a record. It was his vinyl request.

I still remember my first date with my wife. She gave me butterflies— which I thought was a rather odd gift.

I got my first date of the year lined up. It's a court date, but, hey, it's still a date—and I'm dressing up.

My daughter thinks I don't give her enough privacy. At least, that's what she wrote in her diary.

"Life is short... break the rules, forgive quickly, kiss slowly, love truly, laugh uncontrollably, and never regret anything that made you smile." (Mae West)

I ordered a chicken and an egg from Amazon. Let's see which comes first.

Turning vegan would be a big missed steak.

Crushing pop cans is soda pressing.

I have a chicken—proof lawn. It's impeccable.

I ate a frozen apple. Hard core.

When the smog lifts in California, UCLA.

I hate this snow! No... wait... I love this snow! Signed, Bi-Polar Bear

Beer nuts for sale — $1.25 per bag. Deer nuts are under a buck.

I'm terrified of elevators and I'm taking steps to avoid them.

Drink wine. It isn't good to keep things bottled up.

People are making apocalypse jokes like there's no tomorrow.

Cows have hooves because they lactose.

I'm friends with 25 letters of the alphabet. I don't know Y.

For chemists, alcohol is not a problem, it's a solution.

My relationship with whiskey is on the rocks.

Puns about communism aren't funny unless everyone gets them.

Whenever I try to eat healthy, a chocolate bar looks at me and Snickers.

Electricians have to strip to make ends meet.

Well, to be Frank, I'd have to change my name.

Dogs can't operate MRI scanners, but Catscan.

"For Christmas one year I bought my son a BB gun. He bought me a t—shirt with a bull's eye on the back." (Rodney Dangerfield)

Our mountains aren't just funny, they're hill areas.

Life and beer are very similar. Chill for best results.

A cow stumbles into pot field. The steaks have never been higher.

"I never made `Who's Who,' but I'm featured in 'What's That?'" (Phyllis Diller)

Double negatives are a No-No in English.

Irony — the opposite of wrinkly.

The problem with political jokes is that sometimes they get elected.

Forget World Peace. Visualize using your turn signal.

I'm Pining for a good tree pun. I wish they were more Poplar.

Silence is golden. Duct tape is silver.

Afraid of Santa? You may be Claustrophobic.

Sweet dreams are made of cheese. Who am I to dis a brie?

I danced like no one was watching. My court date is pending.

"I've learned that when you harbor bitterness, happiness will dock elsewhere." (Andy Rooney)

"I intend to live forever or die trying." (Groucho Marx)
When my uncle died, he wanted his remains pressed into a record. It was his vinyl request.

I still remember my first date with my wife. She gave me butterflies— which I thought was a rather odd gift.

I got my first date of the year lined up. It's a court date, but, hey, it's still a date—and I'm dressing up.

"There are no good girls gone wrong—just bad girls found out." (Mae West)

My daughter thinks I don't give her enough privacy. At least, that's what she wrote in her diary.

I'm so poor, I can't afford to pay attention.

I'm in shape. (Round is a shape.)

"This woman goes into a gun shop and says, 'I want to buy a gun for my husband.' The clerk says, 'Did he tell you what kind of gun?' 'No,' she replied. 'He doesn't even know I'm going to shoot him.'" (Phyllis Diller)

"You know you're getting old when the candles cost more than the cake." (Bob Hope)

"I didn't get old on purpose; it just happened. If you're lucky, it could happen to you." (Andy Rooney)

"Aging seems to be the only available way to live a long life." (Kitty O'Neill Collins)

"Americans are getting stronger. Twenty years ago, it took two people to carry ten dollars' worth of groceries. Today, a five-year-old can do it." (Henny Youngman)

Light travels faster than sound. This is why some people appear bright until they open their mouths.

I always take life with a grain of salt... plus, a slice of lemon...and a shot of tequila.

I don't have a beer gut. I have a protective covering for my rock-hard abs.

"Be nice to nerds. You may end up working for them. We all could." (Charles Sykes)

"I don't trust children. They're here to replace us." (Stephen Colbert)

"The optimist proclaims that we live in the best of all possible worlds; and the pessimist fears this is true." (James Branch Cabell)

Scientists have recently discovered a food that greatly reduces sex drive. It's called wedding cake.

Among the things that are so simple even a child can operate them are parents.

A Freudian slip is when you say one thing but mean your mother.

Knock, knock. *Who's there?* Nobel. *Nobel who?* Nobel, so I knock knocked.

"As you get older three things happen. The first is your memory goes, and I can't remember the other two." (Norman Wisdom)

Q. How many egomaniacs does it take to screw in a light bulb?
A. One. The egomaniac holds the light bulb while the world revolves around him.

"I've learned that just one person saying to me, 'You've made my day!' makes my day." — Andy Rooney

Life is like a roll of toilet paper. The closer you get to the end, the faster it goes.

Cop: Please step out of the car. Me: I'm too drunk; you get in.

Sometimes, someone unexpected comes into your life out of nowhere, makes your heart race, and changes you forever. We call these people 'cops.'

The older I get, the earlier it gets late.

"My wife and I keep fighting about sex and money. I think she charges me too much." (Rodney Dangerfield)

Remember that moment when you walked into a spider web and suddenly turned into a karate master?

I don't mean to interrupt people. I just randomly remember things and I get really excited.

When one door closes and another door opens, you're probably in prison.

60 might be the new 40 and, but 9:00 PM is the new midnight.

Interviewer: So, tell me about yourself. Me: I'd rather not... I really want this job.

If you're sitting in a public place and a stranger takes the seat next to you, just stare straight ahead and say, 'Did you bring the money?'

I always read my wife's horoscope to see what kind of day I'm going to have.

To get rid of unwanted junk during the holidays, put it in an Amazon box and leave it on your front porch.

Q: How do you milk sheep?
A: Bring out a new iPhone and charge $1000 for it.

Them: What inspires you to get out of bed every morning?
Me: My bladder, mostly.

A police recruit was asked during an exam, What would you do if you had to arrest your own mother? His reply, "Call for backup.'

Wouldn't it be nice if you read a medicine bottle that said... WARNING: May cause permanent weight loss, remove wrinkles, and increase energy.

Q. Why did the mortgage lender go out of business?
A. Lack of interest.

It doesn't seem right to me that only one company makes the game Monopoly.

"I refuse to join any club that would have me as a member." (Groucho Marx)

"I don't think anyone should write their autobiography until after they're dead." (Samuel Goldwyn)

The darkest time in my life was when I couldn't pay my electricity bill. I won $5 million in the lottery. I decided to take a quarter of it and apply it to my mortgage. Now I only have $4,999,999.75 left.

My stomach is FLAT. The 'L' is just silent.

Be Alert! The world needs more Lerts.

My grandfather told me that he got to see the Titanic, and that from the beginning he told the people not to get on board. He knew it was going to sink, but no one listened, and he repeatedly told them... until the minute he got kicked out of the movie theater.

She: Do men still open car doors?
He: How do you think we get inside?

Adam & Eve were the first ones to ignore the Apple terms and conditions.

"My doctor told me to watch my drinking. Now I drink in front of a mirror." (Rodney Dangerfield)

"The only thing my husband and I have in common is that we were married on the same day." (Phyllis Diller)

There are two ways of arguing with a woman. Neither one works.

Exercise makes you look better naked. So does alcohol. Your choice.

I've combined a laxative and alphabet soup. I call it 'Letter Rip'.

"The worst time to have a heart attack is during a game of charades. (Demetri Martin)

"Next time I see you, remind me not to talk to you." (Groucho Marx)

Never put off 'til tomorrow what you can put off indefinitely.

My landlord said she wanted to talk to me about what she calls my ridiculously high power bill. I told her I'd be home all summer and my door is always open.

'Dammit I'm mad' is 'Dammit I'm mad' spelled backwards.

"When it comes to sex, at my age I like threesomes—in case one of us dies." (Rodney Dangerfield)

My wife and I have discovered the secret to making a marriage last. Two times a week, we go to a nice restaurant and have a little wine and good food. She goes Tuesdays, I go Fridays.

You know me. If I ever win the lottery, rest assured that nobody around me will be poor, and I mean that. I will move to a rich neighborhood.

'I have reviewed this case very carefully,' said the divorce court judge, 'and I've decided to give your wife $775 a week.'
'That's very fair, your honor,' the husband replied, 'and every now and then I'll try to send her a few bucks myself.'

Sometimes when you cry, nobody sees your tears. Sometimes when you're hurt, nobody sees your pain. Sometimes when you're sad, nobody sees your sorrow. But fart just one time....

It's OK to mix peas and corn. Just don't call it 'porn.'

It's never too late to start exercising. That's why I'm waiting until later.

I need everyone to wish me luck. I have a meeting at the bank later, and if all goes well, I will be out of debt. I'm so excited I can barely put on my ski mask.

"I intend to live forever — so far, so good." (Steven Wright)

On my way home last night, I was mugged by a thief. He pointed a knife at me and said, 'Your money or your life.' I told him that I am married—so I have no money and no life. We hugged and cried together. It was a beautiful moment.

"Birthdays are good for you. Statistics show that the people who have the most live the longest." (Larry Lorenzoni)

"It's not that I'm afraid to die, I just don't want to be there when it happens." (Woody Allen)

A burglar entered a bedroom, tied up the husband and wife, kissed the wife's ear, and went to the bathroom. The husband said to the wife, 'Satisfy him or he will kill us. Be strong. I love you.' The wife said to the husband, 'He didn't kiss me. He whispered in my ear that he is gay. He needs

Vaseline and I told him it's in the bathroom. Be strong. I love you, too.'

No one told me that when you get a husband, the ears are sold separately.

I used to be a banker, but I lost interest.

At my age, a trail of clothes leading to the bedroom means I dropped them on the way from the dryer.

"The average dog is a nicer person than the average person." (Andy Rooney)

"You know the trouble with real life? There's no danger music." (Jim Carrey)

A friend suggested putting horse manure on my strawberries. I'm never doing that again. I'm going back to whip cream.

Husbands are the best people to share secrets with. They'll never tell anyone because they aren't even listening.

"Don't go around saying the world owes you a living. The world owes you nothing. It was here first." (Mark Twain)

"It's so much easier to suggest solutions when you don't know too much about the problem." (Malcolm Forbes)

Father: Socrates said, 'I am the wisest man alive, for I know one thing... and that is that I know nothing.'
Son: How did he know that?
Father: His wife told him.

"Going to church doesn't make you a Christian any more than going to a garage makes you an automobile." (Billy Sunday)

I yelled COW! at a woman on a bike and she gave me the finger. Then she plowed her bike straight into the cow. I tried.

Never make a woman mad. They can remember stuff that hasn't even happened yet.

Husband: I'm going down to the pub. Put your coat on.
Wife: Ooh. Am I coming?
Husband: No. I'm turning off the heat.

1st Woman: How did you meet your husband?
2nd Woman: I'm a pharmacist. One day he came in to buy condoms and he asked for XXXXXL. It was only after we got married that I realized he stutters.

"Ignorance is preferable to error, and he is less remote from the truth who believes nothing than he who believes what is wrong." (Thomas Jefferson)

Husband: What's for dinner?
Wife: Nothing.
Husband: We had nothing last night.
Wife: I know. I made enough for two days.

Work from home tip: Blowing on the wine in the mug will help convince your zoom meeting that your tea is hot.

"It would be nice if people said, 'God bless you' not just when you sneezed but also when you farted." (Demetri Martin)

Being a little older, I am very fortunate to have someone call and check on me every day. He's from India and he's very concerned about my car warranty.

I said I was good at making decisions. I didn't say the decisions I made were good.

You can't believe everything you hear—but you can repeat it.

Patient: Will I be okay, Doc?
Doctor: I doubt it. Mercury is in Uranus right now.
Patient: I don't do that astrology stuff.
Doctor: Me neither. My thermometer just broke.

The ability to speak several languages is an asset, but the ability to keep your mouth shut in any language is priceless.

"Old age is when you resent the swimsuit issue of Sports Illustrated because there are fewer articles to read." (George Burns)

"A stockbroker urged me to buy a stock that would triple its value every year. I told him, 'At my age, I don't even buy green bananas.'" (Claude Pepper)

A guy walks into a lumberyard and asks for some two-by-fours. The clerk asks, 'How long do you need them?'
The guy answers, 'A long time. We're gonna build a house.'

1st man: Birds poop 27 times a day on average.
2nd man: Wow! I'm sure glad my name's not Average.

You'll always stay young if you live honestly, eat slowly, sleep sufficiently, work industriously, worship faithfully, and lie about your age.

I've written a song about tortillas. Actually, it's more of a rap.

"Life is like a box of chocolates. It doesn't last long if you're fat." (Joe Lycett)

The first time I got a universal remote control, I thought, 'This changes everything!'

"There is nothing like puking with somebody to make you into old friends." (Sylvia Plath)

"Clothes make the man. Naked people have little or no influence in society." (Mark Twain)

"Halloween is the beginning of the holiday shopping season. That's for women. The beginning of the holiday shopping season for men is Christmas Eve." (David Letterman)

"I have never developed indigestion from eating my words." (Winston Churchill)

"A man walks into a chemist's and says, 'Can I have a bar of soap, please?'
The chemist says, 'Do you want it scented?'
And the man says, 'No, thanks. I'll take it with me now.'" (Ronnie Barker)

My girlfriend said, 'You act like a detective too much; I want to split up.' 'Good idea,' I replied. 'We can cover more ground that way.'

About a month before he died, my uncle had his back covered in lard. After that, he went downhill fast.

"It's not the men in my life that count, it's the life in my men." (Mae West)

Went to the zoo. There was only one dog in it. It was a shih tzu.

I'm reading a horror story in Braille. Something bad is about to happen… I can feel it.

My cross-eyed wife and I just got a divorce. I found out she was seeing someone on the side.

"Would I rather be feared or loved? Easy. Both. I want people to be afraid of how much they love me." (Steve Carell as Michael Scott in *The Office*)

"I'm not offended by blonde jokes because I know I'm not dumb. And I also know that I'm not blonde." (Dolly Parton)

"Before you marry a person, you should first make them use a computer with slow Internet service to see who they really are." (Will Ferrell)

"Sometimes I wonder if men and women really suit each other. Perhaps they should just live next door and visit now and then." (Katharine Hepburn)

If it's cold, stay close to others. Otherwise, you might feel a bit ice-olated.

Man: Doc, I can't stop singing *The Green, Green Grass Of Home*.
Doctor: That sounds like Tom Jones syndrome.
Man: Is it common?
Doctor: It's not unusual.

"Employee of the Month is a good example of how somebody can be both a winner and a loser at the same time." (Demetri Martin)

After the Roosevelt Room and the Lincoln Bedroom, Donald Trump said his favorite room in the White House was the Oval Office. He thinks that President Oval was a really great president.

"I could tell my parents hated me. My bath toys were a toaster and a radio." (Rodney Dangerfield)

"I didn't fail the test. I just found 100 ways to do it wrong." (Benjamin Franklin)

I burnt my Hawaiian pizza last night. I should have put it on aloha setting.

My girlfriend told me she was leaving me because I keep pretending to be a Transformer. I said, 'No, wait! I can change.'

Q. What's worse than ants in your pants?
A. uncles

"When I read about the evils of drinking, I gave up reading." (Henny Youngman)

The problem isn't that obesity runs in your family. The problem is that no one runs in your family.

Don't you hate it when someone answers their own questions?
I do.

"I love being married. It's so great to find that one special person you want to annoy for the rest of your life." (Rita Rudner)

"I married for love but the obvious side benefit of having someone around to find my glasses cannot be ignored." (Cameron Esposito)

"Behind every great man is a woman rolling her eyes." (Jim Carrey)

"Marriage is an attempt to solve problems together which you didn't even have when you were on your own." (Eddie Cantor)

I don't have a girlfriend, but I do know a girl that would get really mad if she heard me say that.

Where there's a will... there's a dead person.

"It is better to remain silent and be thought a fool than to speak out and remove all doubt." (Abraham Lincoln)

"There is no sunrise so beautiful that it is worth waking me up to see it." (Mindy Kaling)

A clear conscience is usually the sign of a bad memory.

"Two things are infinite: the universe and human stupidity. And I'm not sure about the former." (Albert Einstein)

All those who believe in psychokinesis raise my hand.

"Gentlemen, you can't fight in here. This is the war room." (Peter Sellers as President Merkin Muffley in *Dr. Strangelove*)

Dancing is a perpendicular expression of a horizontal desire.

I planted some birdseed. A bird came up. Now I don't know what to feed it.

Mechanic: I couldn't repair your brakes, so I made your horn louder.

I took a course in speed waiting. Now I can wait an hour in only ten minutes.

A conclusion is the place where you got tired of thinking.

I've decided to sell my Hoover... it was just collecting dust.

42% of all statistics are made up.

A conscience is what hurts when all your other parts feel so good.

"People say nothing is impossible, but I do nothing every day." (A.A. Milne)

Ambition is a poor excuse for not having enough sense to be lazy.

"Accept who you are... unless you're a serial killer." (Ellen DeGeneres)

"One of the keys to happiness is a bad memory."
(Rita Mae Brown)

"Never go to bed mad. Stay up and fight." (Phyllis Diller)

For every action, there is an equal and opposite criticism.

How do you tell when you're out of invisible ink?

"My husband and I fell in love at first sight. Maybe I should have taken a second look." (Mia Farrow as Halley Reed in *Crimes and Misdemeanors*)

Cross country skiing is great if you live in a small country.

Drugs may lead to nowhere, but at least it's the scenic route.

I went to a general store. They wouldn't let me buy anything specifically.

I bought some powdered water, but I don't know what to add to it.

Everyone has a photographic memory. Some just don't have film.

"Marriage is a wonderful institution, but who wants to live in an institution?" (Groucho Marx)

"Remember, your Valentine's card shows you care enough to send the very best, even though you're too lazy to put it in your own words." (Melanie White)

If you were going to shoot a mime, would you have to use a silencer?

I was trying to daydream, but my mind kept wandering.

"I'd like to have a kid, but I'm not sure I'm ready to spend 10 years of my life constantly asking someone where his shoes are." (Damien Fahey)

"I grew up with six brothers. That's how I learned to dance — waiting for the bathroom." (Bob Hope)

If Barbie is so popular, why do you have to buy her friends?

"A hard man is good to find." (Mae West)

Right now, I'm having amnesia and dйja vu at the same time. I think I've forgotten this before.

Smoking cures weight problems...eventually.

Join the Army, meet interesting people, kill them.

"The only thing worse than being talked about is not being talked about." (Oscar Wilde)

"Never follow anyone else's path. Unless you're in the woods and you're lost, and you see a path.

Then, by all means, follow that path." (Ellen DeGeneres)

Common sense is like deodorant. The people who need it most never use it.

"A woman is like a tea bag—you can't tell how strong she is until you put her in hot water." (Eleanor Roosevelt)

Eagles may soar, but weasels don't get sucked into jet engines.

I almost had a psychic girlfriend, but she left me before we met.

"Thankfully, perseverance is a great substitute for talent." (Steve Martin)

"By the time someone says, 'To make a long story short,' it's too late." (Don Herold)

Bills travel through the mail at twice the speed of checks.

I bought a house on a one-way, dead-end road. I don't know how I got there.

I spilled spot remover on my dog. He's gone now.

"There is no such thing as 'fun for the whole family.'" (Jerry Seinfeld)

"If I'm not back in five minutes, just wait longer."
(Jim Carrey as Ace Ventura in *Ace Ventura: Pet Detective*)

Everywhere is walking distance if you've got the time.

Support bacteria — they're the only culture some people have.

The hardness of the butter is proportional to the softness of the bread.

I used to have an open mind, but my brains kept falling out.

"The only time I set the bar low is for limbo" (Steve Carell as Michael Scott in *The Office*)

"Some family trees bear an enormous crop of nuts." (Wayne Huizenga)

I had amnesia once or twice.

"I love to read. My education is self-inflicted." (Groucho Marx)

My theory of evolution is that Darwin was adopted.

"Happiness is having a large, loving, caring, close-knit family... in another city." (George Burns)

The problem with the gene pool is that there is no lifeguard.

I put instant coffee in a microwave oven and almost went back in time.

There is a fine line between fishing and just standing on the shore like an idiot.

"I want my children to have all the things I couldn't afford. Then I want to move in with them." (Phyllis Diller)

"Children are a great comfort to us in our old age, and they help us reach it faster, too." (John Ruskin)

I got a new dog. He's a paranoid retriever. He brings back everything because he's not sure what I threw him.

"When your mother asks, 'Do you want a piece of advice?' it's a mere formality. It doesn't matter if you answer yes or no. You're going to get it anyway." (Erma Bombeck)

I'd kill for a Nobel Peace Prize.

"My father had a profound influence on me. He was a lunatic." (Spike Milligan)

"The other night I ate at a real nice family restaurant. Every table had an argument going." — George Carlin

What a nice night for an evening.

When everything is coming your way, you're in the wrong lane.

Why do psychics have to ask you for your name?

Monday is an awful way to spend 1/7th of your life.

"A hospital bed is a parked taxi with the meter running." (Groucho Marx)

Depression is merely anger without enthusiasm.

I was a peripheral visionary. I could see the future, but only way off to the side.

"I'm addicted to placebos." (Steven Wright)

A friend of mine once sent me a postcard with a picture of the entire planet Earth taken from space. On the back, it said, 'Wish you were here.'

"People often say that motivation doesn't last. Well, neither does bathing; that's why we recommend it daily." (Zig Ziglar)

"Life is like a sewer — what you get out of it depends on what you put into it." (Tom Lehrer)

I saw a subliminal advertising executive, but only for a second.

"If it wasn't for pickpockets, I'd have no sex life at all." (Rodney Dangerfield)

Do Lipton employees take coffee breaks?

What happens if you get scared half to death twice?

I'm writing an unauthorized autobiography.

"When I was a kid, we were so poor that if I hadn't been a boy I wouldn't have had anything to play with." (Rodney Dangerfield)

Even snakes are afraid of snakes.

When I was in school the teachers told me practice makes perfect; then they told me nobody's perfect, so I stopped practicing.

I bought some batteries, but they weren't included.

I hate it when my foot falls asleep during the day because that means it's going to be up all night.

I invented the cordless extension cord.

"I generally avoid temptation unless I can't resist it." (Mae West)

I have a hobby. I have the world's largest collection of seashells. I keep it scattered on beaches all over the world. Maybe you've seen some of it.

A lot of people are afraid of heights. Not me. I'm afraid of widths.

I was going 70 miles an hour and got stopped by a cop who said, 'Do you know the speed limit is 55 miles per hour?' 'Yes, officer,' I said, 'but I wasn't going to be out that long....'

I went to a fancy French restaurant called *Déjà Vu*. The headwaiter said, 'Don't I know you?'

What's another word for Thesaurus?

I went to a restaurant that serves breakfast at any time. I ordered French Toast during the Renaissance.

"All I can say is that I have taken more out of alcohol than alcohol has taken out of me."
(Winston Churchill)

I used to have superpowers but the psychiatrist took them all away.

If you think nobody cares about you, just try missing a couple of payments.

"I know worrying works, because none of the stuff I worried about ever happened." (Will Rogers)

"The 50—50—90 rule: Anytime you have a 50—50 chance of getting something right, there's a 90% probability you'll get it wrong." (Andy Rooney)

"I saved a girl from being attacked last night. I controlled myself." (Rodney Dangerfield)

What is the speed of dark?

I have an answering machine in my car. It says, 'I'm home now. But leave a message, and I'll call when I'm out.'

I worked in a health food store once. A guy came in and asked me, 'If I melt dry ice, can I take a bath without getting wet?'

"I'm a woman of very few words, but lots of action." (Mae West)

Why is it that you can wave a fan, and you can wave a club, but you can't wave a fan club?

You can't have everything. Where would you put it?

Change is inevitable.... except from vending machines.

"Do you remember the first time you had sex? I do, and boy, was I scared! I was alone!" (Rodney Dangerfield)

"Even if you are on the right track, you'll get run over if you just sit there." (Will Rogers)

Light travels faster than sound. This is why some people appear bright until you hear them speak.

Q: I am there once a minute, twice in a moment but never in a thousand years. What am I?
A: The letter 'M.'

"Be who you are and say what you feel, because those who mind don't matter and those who matter don't mind." (Bernard Baruch)

I used to work in a fire hydrant factory. You couldn't park anywhere near the place.

It's a small world, but I wouldn't want to have to paint it.

"I've been asked to say a couple of words about my husband. How about short and cheap?"
(Phyllis Diller)

"His mother should have thrown him out and kept the stork." (Mae West)

Plan to be spontaneous tomorrow.

Experience is something you don't get until just after you need it.

Half the people you know are below average.

The sooner you fall behind, the more time you'll have to catch up.

"A couple just married were happy with the whole thing. He was happy with the *hole*, and she was happy with the *thing*." (Andy Rooney)

Q. What do you call a can opener that doesn't work?
work?
A. A *can't* opener.

"The important thing to remember is not to forget." (Benny Bellamacina)

"The minute you settle for less than you deserve, you get even less than you settled for." (Maureen Dowd)

"I've got all the money I'll ever need—if I die by 4 o'clock." (Henny Youngman)

To steal ideas from one person is plagiarism; to steal from many is research.

The early bird gets the worm, but the second mouse gets the cheese.

"One man with conviction will overwhelm a hundred who have only opinions." (Winston Churchill)

"If sex is a pain in the ass, then you're doing it wrong." (Rodney Dangerfield)

A blind man walked into a bar... and a table... and a chair....

Q. What do you call a fish with no eye?
A. Fsh.

If everything seems to be going well, you've obviously overlooked something.

"When you come to a fork in the road.... take it." (Yogi Berra)

"When I'm good, I'm very good. But when I'm bad I'm better." (Mae West)

Pollen is what happens when flowers can't keep it in their plants.

I can tell when people are being judgmental just by looking at them.

Q. What do you get when you cross a rooster with an owl?
A. A cock that stays up all night.

"Outside of a dog, a book is a man's best friend. Inside of a dog it's too dark to read." (Groucho Marx)

"Remarrying a husband you've divorced is like having your appendix put back in." (Phyllis Diller)

"Some cause happiness wherever they go; others whenever they go." (Oscar Wilde)

Most people are shocked when they find out how bad I am as an electrician.

I told my girlfriend she drew her eyebrows too high. She seemed surprised.

Always borrow money from pessimists—they don't expect it back.

Hard work pays off in the future. Laziness pays off now.

If I wanted to hear from an asshole, I'd fart.

Q. Why was the shark model in *Jaws* called 'Bruce'?
A. Because Steven Spielberg named it after his lawyer.

"I have made good judgments in the past. I have made good judgments in the future." (Dan Quayle)

"When I was a kid, my parents moved a lot, but I always found them." (Rodney Dangerfield)

I'm reading a book about anti-gravity. It's impossible to put down.

Yesterday, I accidentally swallowed some food coloring. The doctor says I'm okay, but I feel like I've dyed a little inside.

"My mother never breast fed me. She told me she only liked me as a friend." (Rodney Dangerfield)

"Experience is simply the name we give our mistakes." (Oscar Wilde)

Not in jail, not in a mental hospital, not in a grave—I'd say I'm having a very good day.

"If at first you don't succeed... so much for skydiving." (Henny Youngman)

I wrote a song, but I can't read music, so I don't know what it is. Every once in a while, I'll be listening to the radio, and I say, 'I think I might have written that.'

The severity of the itch is proportional to the reach.

One time, a cop pulled me over for running a stop sign. He said, 'Didn't you see the stop sign?' I said, 'Yeah, but I don't believe everything I read.'

Sponges grow in the ocean. I wonder how much deeper the ocean would be without them.

When I was a kid, we had a sandbox. It was a quicksand box. I was an only child...eventually.

"I was so ugly my mother used to feed me with a sling shot." (Rodney Dangerfield)

"For every complex problem, there is a solution that is simple, neat, and wrong." (H. L. Mencken)

I was riding a donkey the other day when someone threw a rock at me, and I fell off. I guess I was stoned off my ass.

Q. What's the difference between ignorance and apathy?
A. I don't know, and I don't care.

Ever notice how irons have a setting for permanent press? I don't get it...

"We are ready for any unforeseen event that may or may not occur." (Dan Quayle)

"Failure is the condiment that gives success its flavor." (Truman Capote)

"Never let your sense of morals prevent you from doing what is right." (Isaac Asimov)

"If you're going to be able to look back on something and laugh about it, you might as well laugh about it now." (Marie Osmond)

"I have a simple philosophy: Fill what is empty. Empty what is full. Scratch where it itches." (Alice Roosevelt Longworth)

Q. Why can't a nose be 12 inches long?
A. Because then it would be a foot.

My luck is like a bald guy who just won a comb.

"Even a stopped clock is right twice every day. After some years, it can boast of a long series of successes." (Marie von Ebner-Eschenbach)

"You must learn from the mistakes of others. You can't possibly live long enough to make them all yourself." (Sam Levenson)

"Honest criticism is hard to take, particularly from a relative, a friend, an acquaintance, or a stranger." (Franklin P. Jones)

I got a new pair of gloves today, but they're both 'lefts,' which on the one hand is great, but on the other, it's just not right.

"Whenever I see a man with a beard, moustache and glasses, I think, 'There's a man who has taken every precaution to avoid people doodling on photographs of him.'" (Carey Marx)

An ergasiophobe is someone who's afraid of work.

'Doctor, there's a patient on line one that says he's invisible.'
'Well, tell him I can't see him right now.'

Someday you'll go far. I hope you stay there.

So what if I don't know what apocalypse means? It's not the end of the world!

"My mother had morning sickness *after* I was born." (Rodney Dangerfield)

"The best argument against democracy is a five-minute conversation with the average voter." (Winston Churchill)

"Only the shallow know themselves." (Oscar Wilde)

I want a job cleaning mirrors. It's something I can really see myself doing.

I failed math so many times at school, I can't even count.

A giraffe's coffee would be cold by the time it reached the bottom of its throat. Ever think about that? No, you only think about yourself.

My kids say they want a cat for Christmas. Normally I serve turkey, but, hey, if it will make them happy....

WIFE to HUSBAND: 'Sure, I make terrible choices. One of them was you.'

"My grandmother is over eighty and she still doesn't need glasses. Drinks right out of the bottle." (Henny Youngman)

"It's time for the human race to enter the solar system." (Dan Quayle)

Sometimes I wake up grumpy; other times I let him sleep.

I work 40 hours a week to be this poor.

Towing company motto: We don't charge an arm and a leg. We just want your tows.

I can please only one person per day. Today is not your day. Tomorrow, isn't looking good either.

"Despite the old saying, 'Don't take your troubles to bed', many men still sleep with their wives!" (Andy Rooney)

"A fanatic is one who can't change his mind and won't change the subject." (Winston Churchill)

"Slump? I ain't in no slump... I just ain't hitting." (Yogi Berra)

"Here's to our wives and girlfriends...may they never meet!" (Groucho Marx)

"Looking 50 is great... if you're 60." (Joan Rivers)

I just burned 1,200 calories. I forgot the pizza in the oven.

Who knew that the hardest thing of being an adult is figuring out what to fix for dinner and doing it every single night for the rest of your life until you die?

I hate it when people act all intellectual and talk about Mozart, when they've never even seen one of his paintings.

Never trust an electrician with no eyebrows.

"During sex, my girlfriend always wants to talk to me. Just the other night she called me from a hotel." (Rodney Dangerfield)

"Whatever it is, I'm against it." (Groucho Marx)

Doctor: I'm just waiting for your x-ray.
Blonde: But I've never dated anyone named 'Ray'.
Doctor: And we might do a brain scan, too...

I know, by saying that, that I'm dating myself—but we're thinking about breaking up.

"Getting married is like trading the adoration of many for the sarcasm of one." (Mae West)

I try to see the best in people, but you certainly make it hard.

Never criticize a man until you've walked a mile in his shoes. That way, if he doesn't like what you have to say, you're a mile away and you have his shoes.

Tact is for people who aren't witty enough to be sarcastic.

Marriage is when a man and woman become as one; the trouble starts when they try to decide which one.

It's funny, when I walk into a spider web, I demolish his home and interrupt his dinner, yet I still feel like the victim.

"You can't have everything. Where would you put it? (Steven Wright)

Not to brag, but I already have a date for Valentine's Day — Feb. 14.

When I heard that oxygen and magnesium were dating, I was like OMg.

Did you hear about the notebook that married the pencil? She finally found Mr. Write.

"It does not matter whether you win or lose, what matters is whether I win or lose!" (Steven Weinberg)

"If you think you are too small to be effective, you've never been in the dark with a mosquito." (Betty Reese)

"Today's opportunities erase yesterday's failures." (Gene Brown)

Everybody is born with genius, but most people only keep it a few minutes.

Summer is the season when a man thinks he can cook better on an outdoor grill than his wife can on an indoor stove.

We're all brothers and sisters, we just have different mothers and fathers.

The voices in my head may not be real, but they have some good ideas!

I love to go shopping. I love to freak out salespeople. They ask me if they can help me, and I say, 'Have you got anything I'd like?' Then they ask me what size I need, and I say, 'Extra medium.'

There was a kidnapping at school yesterday. Don't worry, though — he woke up!

I make apocalypse jokes like there's no tomorrow.

"Most people are other people. Their thoughts are someone else's opinions, their lives a mimicry, their passions a quotation." (Oscar Wilde)

A recent study has found that women who carry a little extra weight live longer than the men who mention it.

"Even if you are on the right track, you will get run over if you just sit there." (Will Rogers)

"If a cluttered desk is a sign of a cluttered mind, of what, then, is an empty desk a sign?" (Albert Einstein)

"Things work out best for those who make the best of how things work out." (John Wooden)

"Whoever said, 'It's not whether you win or lose that counts' probably lost." (Martina Navratilova)

Love is grand; divorce is a hundred grand.

If you are going to be blue, be bright blue!

You always find things in the last place you look... unless you're stupid enough to keep looking after you find them.

You have a right to your opinions. I just don't want to hear them.

I'm trying to imagine you with a personality.

Out to lunch: If not back by five, out for dinner also.

"There are no traffic jams along the extra mile." (Roger Staubach)

"Ambition is a poor excuse for not having sense enough to be lazy." (Charlie McCarthy)

"A man who correctly guesses a woman's age may be smart, but he's not very bright." (Lucille Ball)

"There's never enough time to do all the nothing you want." (Bill Watterson)

You only live once, but if you do it right, once is enough.

Those who are easily shocked should be shocked more often.

Give a man a free hand and he'll run it all over you.

Sex is emotion in motion.

Q: What happened when the marsupial applied for a mortgage? A: He didn't koalafy.

Trapezoid — A device for catching zoids.

"Life isn't finding shelter in the storm. It's about learning to dance in the rain." (Sherrilyn Kenyon)

Askhole: A person that constantly asks for advice, yet always does the complete opposite of what you advised them to do,

"When everyone thinks alike, no one thinks very much." (Walter Lippmann)

"My cousin's gay. He went to London only to find out that Big Ben was a clock." (Rodney Dangerfield)

When life gives you melons, you might be dyslexic.

You're the reason God created the middle finger.

Q. What kind of drink can be bitter and sweet?
A. Reali—tea.

"The only way to get rid of temptation is to yield to it. I can resist everything but temptation." (Oscar Wilde)

I want to be cremated when I die. It's my last hope for a smoking hot body.

"Do you know what it means to come home at night to a woman who'll give you a little love, a little affection, a little tenderness? It means you're in the wrong house; that's what it means." (Henny Youngman)

"Women want mediocre men, and men are working hard to be as mediocre as possible." (Margaret Mead)

There may be no 'I' in team, but there is a 'ME.'

The light at the end of the tunnel is sometimes an oncoming train.

You have to be 100% behind someone before you can stab them in the back.

If you can keep your head when all around you have lost theirs, then you probably haven't understood the seriousness of the situation.

"A hooker once told me she had a headache." (Rodney Dangerfield)

"Who discovered we could get milk from cows and what did he think he was doing at the time?" (Bill Connolly)

Does killing time damage eternity?

"A bachelor is a guy who never made the same mistake once." (Phyllis Diller)

"I never forget a face, but in your case, I'll be glad to make an exception." (Groucho Marx)

Need an ark to save two of every animal? I Noah guy.

Did you hear the one about the cross-eyed teacher who couldn't control his pupils?

I hear the action at the circus was in tents.

I told my niece that I saw a moose on the way to work this morning. She said, "How do you know he has a job?"

"True friends stab you in the front." (Oscar Wilde)

Numbers that can't be divided by two seem odd to me.

If it looks like shit, smells like shit, and feels like shit, you don't have to taste it.

Geology rocks but geography is where it's at!

"Some men change their party for the sake of their principles; others their principles for the sake of their party." (Winston Churchill)

Q: How did the picture end up in jail?
A: It was framed!

I do not have Alzheimer's. I have 'Some-timers.' Sometimes I remember and sometimes I don't.

"I feel sorry for short people, you know. When it rains, they're the last to know." (Rodney Dangerfield)

"When I want your opinion, I'll give it to you." (Samuel Goldwyn)

Walking can add minutes to your life. This enables you, at 85 years old, to spend an additional 5 months in a nursing home at $7000 per month.

I want to be 14 again and ruin my life differently. I have new ideas.

"Women like a man with a past, but they prefer a man with a present." (Mae West)

Apparently RSVP'ing to a wedding invitation with 'Maybe next time' isn't the correct response.

So my neighbor knocked on my front door at 3 am. 3AM!!! Luckily, I was already up playing the bagpipes.

"His finest hour lasted a minute and a half." (Phyllis Diller)

Instead of cleaning my house, I just watch an episode of The Hoarders, and think, 'Wow! My house looks great.'

If God is watching us, the least we can do is be entertaining.

It's weird being the same age as old people.

"The problem with doing nothing is that you never know when you're finished." (Groucho Marx)

"A clear conscience is a sure sign of a bad memory." (Mark Twain)

People who ask me what I'm doing tomorrow probably assume that I even know what day of the week it is.

"It's true hard work never killed anybody, but I figure, why take the chance?" (Ronald Reagan)

"I know that there are people who do not love their fellow man, and I hate people like that!" (Tom Lehrer)

Knowledge is knowing a tomato is a fruit. Wisdom is not putting it in a fruit salad.

A computer once beat me at chess, but it was no match for me at kickboxing.

Give a man a fish and you feed him for a day. But teach a man to fish, and he will sit in a boat and drink beer all day.

"You've got to be very careful if you don't know where you are going, because you might not get there." (Yogi Berra)

There are three kinds of people: those who can count and those who can't.

When I was young, I was poor. But after years of hard work, I am no longer young.

I don't have the energy to pretend to like you right now.

Being opinionated is not the same as being informed.

"I love California. I practically grew up in Phoenix." (Dan Quayle)

You remind me of a penny. Two-faced and not worth much.

"The future ain't what it used to be." (Yogi Berra)

"I figured out I'm bisexual. I have sex twice a year." (Rodney Dangerfield)

"Good girls go to heaven; bad girls go everywhere." (Mae West)

It's impossible to joke around with a kleptomaniac. They always take things… literally.

Q: Why aren't dogs good dancers?
A: Because they have two left feet.

"Just got back from a pleasure trip: I took my mother-in-law to the airport." (Henny Youngman)

Regular naps prevent old age, especially if you take them while driving.

"He's so old that when he orders a 3-minute egg, they ask for the money upfront." (George Burns)

"By the time a man is wise enough to watch his step, he's too old to go anywhere." (Billy Crystal)

"I'm sitting on top of the world, and I've got hemorrhoids." (Rodney Dangerfield)

My favorite word is drool. It just rolls off the tongue.

"I tried phone sex once, but the holes in the dial were too small." (Andy Rooney)

"A lady came up to me one day and said 'Sir! You are drunk'!' to which I replied, 'I am drunk today, Madam, and tomorrow I shall be sober, but you will still be ugly." (Winston Churchill)

"Between two evils, I always pick the one I never tried before." (Mae West)

I'm not responsible for what my face does when you talk.

I'm at that age where my mind still thinks I'm 29; my humor suggests I'm 12 while my body mostly keeps asking if I'm sure I'm not dead yet.

Q: How is a boiled noodle like a man with EDS?
A: No hard feelings.

I asked myself if I was crazy and we all said 'No.'

"For NASA, space is still a high priority." (Dan Quayle)

"I'll believe color television when I see it in black and white." (Samuel Goldwyn)

You're confusing me with someone who cares what you think.

"I never let schooling interfere with my education." (Mark Twain)

I see people around my age mountain climbing; I feel good getting my leg through my underwear without losing my balance.

I believe we should all pay our tax bill with a smile. I tried but they wanted cash.

I'm feeling pretty proud of myself. The puzzle I bought said '3-5 years', but I finished it in 18 months.

There are three kinds of people—those who can count and those who can't.

"What have future generations ever done for us?" (Groucho Marx)

"I never said most of the things I said." (Yogi Berra)

"My uncle's dying wish — he wanted me on his lap. He was in the electric chair." (Rodney Dangerfield)

You know when people say, 'It's always the last place you look.' Of course, it is. Why would you keep looking after you've found it?

"If you can't give me your word of honor, will you give me your promise?" (Samuel Goldwyn)

My grandpa started walking five miles a day when he was 60.
Now he's 97 years old and we don't know where he is.

"Everyone has his day, and some days last longer than others." (Winston Churchill)

I like long walks, especially when they are taken by people who annoy me.

The only reason I would take up walking is so that I could hear heavy breathing again.

"Out of intense complexities, intense simplicities emerge." (Winston Churchill)

"A self-taught man usually has a poor teacher and a worse student." (Henny Youngman)

"A man's only as old as the woman he feels."
(Groucho Marx)

At my age, the only pole dancing I do is to hold on to the safety bar in the bathtub.

"Question: What's an Australian kiss? Answer: The same thing as a French kiss, only down under."
(Andy Rooney)

"All you need in this life is ignorance and confidence, and then success is sure." (Mark Twain)

"Luck is what you have left over after you give 100 percent." (Langston Coleman)

This is my step ladder. I never knew my real ladder.

I am not a vegetarian because I love animals. I am a vegetarian because I hate plants.

I hate Russian dolls; they're so full of themselves.

I don't suffer from insanity. I enjoy every minute of it.

Just burned 2,000 calories. That's the last time I leave brownies in the oven while I nap.

My boss is going to fire the employee with the worst posture. I have a hunch it might be me.

When I lose the TV controller, it's always hidden in some remote destination.

"Marriage is the only war where you get to sleep with the enemy." (Andy Rooney)

"I find television very educational. Every time someone turns it on, I go in the other room and read a book." (Groucho Marx)

"A verbal contract isn't worth the paper it's written on." (Samuel Goldwyn)

"The best contraceptive for old people is nudity." (Phyllis Diller)

"No one goes there nowadays; it's too crowded." (Yogi Berra)

Something about subtraction just doesn't add up.

Keep talking. I always yawn when I'm interested.

Don't criticize my mess unless you'd like to become part of it.

You need to learn to accept imperfection... and I can help you with that.

"Diplomacy is the art of telling people to go to hell in such a way that they ask for directions." (Winston Churchill)

"I always thought the record would stand until it was broken." (Yogi Berra)

"Question: What are the three biggest tragedies in a man's life? Answer: Life sucks. Job sucks. Wife doesn't." (Andy Rooney)

Light travels faster than sound. That's why some people appear bright until they open their mouths.

If you arrest a mime, do you have to tell him he has the right to remain silent?

Four fonts walk into a bar. The bartender says, "Hey, get out. We don't want your type in here."

Money talks. But all mine ever says is goodbye.

"A heifer cow is better than none, but this is no time for puns." (Groucho Marx)

"My therapist told me the way to achieve true inner peace is to finish what I start. So far, I've finished two bags of M&Ms and a chocolate cake. I feel better already." (Dave Barry)

"Life is a shipwreck, but we must not forget tossing in the lifeboats." (Voltaire)

I think politicians and diapers have one thing in common. They should both be changed regularly and for the same reason.

"Group sex? Are you kidding? I had group sex — my wife screwed me in front of the jury." (Rodney Dangerfield)

"Age is a high price to pay for maturity." (Tom Stoppard)

Some cause happiness wherever they go. Others... whenever they go.

"You take care and I hope I'll run into you — when I'm driving." (Rodney Dangerfield)

"[Mrs. Teasdale]: He's had a change of heart. [Groucho]: A lot of good that'll do him. He's still got the same face." (Groucho Marx)

I asked God for a bike, but I know God doesn't work that way. So I stole a bike and asked for forgiveness.

We live in a society where pizza gets to your house faster than the police.

"It takes considerable knowledge just to realize the extent of your own ignorance." (Thomas Sowell)

"Every man is guilty of all the good he did not do." (Voltaire)

"Women who seek to be equal with men lack ambition." (Marilyn Monroe)

I don't let my age define me, but the side-effects are getting harder to ignore.

"I don't feel old. I don't feel anything until noon. Then it's time for my nap." (Bob Hope)

"Middle age is when a guy starts turning off lights for economic rather than romantic reasons." (Eli Cass)

Growing old is mandatory, but growing up is optional.

"The question isn't who is going to let me; it's who is going to stop me." (Ayn Rand)

"I am an early bird and a night owl… so I am wise, and I have worms." (Michael Scott on *The Office*)

"To steal ideas from one person is plagiarism; to steal from many is research." (Steven Wright)

"I was so ugly my parents had to hang a pork chop around my neck to get the dog to play with me." (Rodney Dangerfield)

"A rich man is nothing but a poor man with money." (W.C. Fields)

I saw a parade of rabbits hopping backward. It was crazy, I've never seen a receding hare line like that.

I saw a bear with no teeth the other day. His friends kept calling him Gummy Bear.

"From the moment I picked your book up until I laid it down, I was convulsed with laughter. Someday I intend reading it." (Groucho Marx)

Did you see that illegally parked frog get toad away?

Today a man knocked on my door and asked for a small donation toward the local swimming pool. I gave him a glass of water.

Did you hear about the guy who got hit in the head with a can of soda? He was lucky it was a soft drink.

"Why do they call it rush hour when nothing moves?" (Robin Williams)

"My father gave me a bat for Christmas. The first time I tried to play with it, it flew away." (Rodney Dangerfield)

"There are only two four letter words that are offensive to men — 'don't' and 'stop', unless they are used together." (Andy Rooney)

If supermarkets are lowering prices every day, why isn't anything in the store free yet?

I got kicked out of a secret cooking society. I spilled the beans.

People who use selfie sticks really need to have a good, long look at themselves.

"Now there's a man with an open mind — you can feel the breeze from here!" (Groucho Marx)

"I believe that if life gives you lemons, you should make lemonade... and try to find somebody whose life has given them vodka and have a party." (Ron White)

I used to think I was indecisive... but now I'm not so sure.

Q: What do you call a guy who's had too much to drink?
A: A cab.

"A man walks into a library and says, 'I hope you don't have a book on reverse psychology.'" (Henny Youngman)

You will also enjoy our article on playing dumb quotes.

"He who laughs last didn't get the joke." (Charles de Gaulle)

"Education is learning what you didn't even know you didn't know." (Daniel J. Boorstin)

"We never really grow up. We only learn how to act in public." (Bryan White)

"I'm not crazy about reality, but it's still the only place to get a decent meal." (Groucho Marx)

I was wondering why the frisbee kept getting bigger and bigger, but then it hit me.

"I say 'no' to drugs. Whenever someone asks me for some of my drugs I say, 'No.'" (Rodney Dangerfield)

I buy all my guns from a guy called T-Rex. He's a small arms dealer.

"Wanting to be someone else is a waste of who you are." (Kurt Cobain)

We all make choices in life but in the end, our choices make us.

"We all die. The goal isn't to live forever. The goal is to create something that will." (Chuck Palahniuk)

"A wife is a sex object. Every time you ask for sex, she objects." (Andy Rooney)

"It's wonderful to be here in the great state of Chicago." (Dan Quayle)

"My fake plants died because I did not pretend to water them." (Mitch Hedberg)

"You must pay for your sins. If you have already paid, please ignore this notice." (Sam Levenson)

I'm reading a book about anti-gravity - it's impossible to put down.

Maybe if we start telling people their brain is an app, they'll want to use it.

"While money can't buy happiness, it certainly lets you choose your own form of misery." (Groucho Marx)

"I come from a stupid family. During the civil war my great uncle fought for the west." (Rodney Dangerfield)

I got a new pair of gloves today, but they're both 'lefts,' which on the one hand is great, but on the other, it's just not right.

"Baseball is 90% mental; the other half is physical." (Yogi Berra)

"If you smile when no one else is around, you really mean it." (Andy Rooney)

A book fell on my head the other day, I only have my shelf to blame.

I went to a seafood disco last week but ended up pulling a mussel.

What did our parents do to kill boredom before the internet? I asked my 26 brothers and sisters, and they didn't know either.

I tried donating blood today...Never again! Too many stupid questions: Whose blood is it? Where did you get it from? Why is it in a bucket?

Learn from your parents' mistakes; use birth control.

"When I played in the sandbox, the cat kept covering me up." (Rodney Dangerfield"

"I can see you in the kitchen bending over a hot stove, and I can't see the stove." (Groucho Marx)

"Question: Why do men find it difficult to make eye contact? Answer: Breasts don't have eyes." (Andy Rooney)

"If you don't know where you are going, you might wind up someplace else." (Yogi Berra)

"Opportunity does not knock; it presents itself when you beat down the door." (Kyle Chandler)

"We don't stop playing because we grow old; we grow old because we stop playing." (George Bernard Shaw)

"The elevator to success is out of order. You'll have to use the stairs… one step at a time." (Joe Girard)

"The difference between genius and stupidity is— genius has its limits." (Albert Einstein)

"Is that a gun in your pocket, or are you just happy to see me?" (Mae West)

"When I hear somebody sigh, 'Life is hard,' I am always tempted to ask, 'Compared to what?'" (Sydney Harris)

"The brain is a wonderful organ; it starts working the moment you get up in the morning and does not stop until you get into the office." (Robert Frost)

"Age is of no importance unless you're a cheese." (Billie Burke)

It's lonely at the top, but you eat better.

Salad is what my dinner eats for dinner.

There are no stupid questions, just stupid people.

Well, by all means, illuminate me.

I'm not your type. I'm not inflatable.

"A bum came up to me saying, I haven't eaten in two days! I said, 'You should force yourself!'"
(Henny Youngman)

"Quite frankly, teachers are the only profession that teach our children." (Dan Quayle)

Don't treat me any differently than you would the Queen.

"The Alps are a simple folk, living on a diet of old shoes. And the Lord Alps those who alp themselves." (Groucho Marx)

"My brother-in-law died. He was a karate expert, then joined the army. The first time he saluted, he killed himself." (Henny Youngman)

So many cats, so few recipes.

Honk if you love peace and quiet.

"I had a date with an inflatable girl. Now I got an inflatable guy looking for me." — Rodney Dangerfield

Do you ever get up in the morning, look in the mirror and think, 'That can't be accurate!'

When one door opens and another closes, you're probably in prison.

"Anyone who goes to see a psychiatrist ought to have his head examined." (Samuel Goldwyn)

"Too much of a good thing can be wonderful." (Mae West)

Children in the back seat cause accidents; accidents in the back seat cause children!

I'd like to help you out. Which way did you come in?

Experience is a wonderful thing. It enables you to recognize a mistake when you make it again.

"If there are no stupid questions, then what kind of questions do stupid people ask? Do they get smart just in time to ask questions?" (Scott Adams)

"Trying is the first step toward failure." (Homer Simpson)

"You will never reach your destination if you stop and throw stones at every dog that barks." (Winston Churchill)

"What you do speaks so loud that I cannot hear what you say." (Ralph Waldo Emerson)

"Life shrinks or expands in proportion to one's courage." (Anais Nin)

"I knew I was going to take the wrong train, so I left early." (Yogi Berra)

"I generally avoid temptation unless I can't resist it." (Mae West)

"The trouble with the rat-race is that, even if you win, you're still a rat." (Lily Tomlin)

"I wish you'd keep my hands to yourself." (Groucho Marx)

"When my old man wanted sex, my mother would show him a picture of me." (Rodney Dangerfield)

"Success consists of going from failure to failure without loss of enthusiasm." (Winston Churchill)

Shoutout to everyone who can still remember their childhood phone number but can't remember the password they created yesterday. You are my people.

My imaginary friend thinks you have serious mental problems.

Silence is golden. Duct tape is silver.

One minute you're young and fun. And next, you're turning down the stereo in your car to see better.

"A person who *won't* read has no advantage over one who *can't* read." (Mark Twain)

What doesn't kill you can only disappoint me.

"A pessimist sees the difficulty in every opportunity; an optimist sees the opportunity in every difficulty." (Winston Churchill)

"I remember the first time I had sex — I kept the receipt." (Groucho Marx)

"You can observe a lot by just watching." (Yogi Berra)

"I'm taking Viagra and drinking prune juice. I don't know if I'm coming or going. (Rodney Dangerfield)

"You take the United Negro College Fund model—that what a waste it is to lose one's mind, or not to have a mind is being very wasteful. How true that is." (Dan Quayle)

"The score never interested me, only the game." (Mae West)

"To succeed in life, you need three things: a wishbone, a backbone and a funny bone." (Reba McEntire)

"A mind is like a parachute. It doesn't work if it's not open." (Frank Zappa)

Jesus loves you ...but I'm his favorite.

I started at the bottom, and it's been downhill ever since.

I got gas today for $1.39. Unfortunately, it was at Taco Bell.

If you want to change the world, do it while you're single. Once you're married you can't even change the TV channel.

I'm never on schedule, but always on time.

Things always go according to plan…when you're making it up as you go along.

"In theory there is no difference between theory and practice. In practice there is." (Yogi Berra)

"Love conquers all things except poverty and toothaches." (Mae West)

"My wife and I were happy for 20 years. Then we met." (Rodney Dangerfield)

"I once wanted to become an atheist, but I gave up. They have no holidays." (Henny Youngman)

I'm at that stage in life where getting LUCKY means going into another room and remembering why I went in there.

"Money won't buy happiness, but it will pay the salaries of a large research staff to study the problem." (Bill Vaughan)

"I think you can destroy your now by worrying about tomorrow." (Janis Joplin)

"Friendship is like peeing on yourself: everyone can see it, but only you get the warm feeling that it brings." (Robert Bloch)

"Pair up in threes." (Yogi Berra)

"I'm not superstitious, but I am a little stitious." (Michael Scott in *The Office*)

"You know you've reached middle age when you're cautioned to slow down by your doctor, instead of by the police." (Joan Rivers)

Truth hurts. Maybe not as much as jumping on a bicycle with a seat missing, but it hurts.

"I used to sell furniture for a living. The trouble was it was my own." (Les Dawson)

I wasn't being rude. I just said what everyone else was thinking.

Q: What would you call someone with just a nose and no body?
A: Nobody knows.

"When I was born, I was given a choice — a big pecker or a good memory.... I don't remember which I chose." (Andy Rooney)

"We make a living by what we get, but we make a life by what we give." (Winston Churchill)

"Time flies like an arrow; fruit flies like a banana." (Groucho Marx)

"I found there was only one way to look thin: hang out with fat people." (Rodney Dangerfield)

I used to have a handle on life, but then it broke.

Never trust atoms; they make up everything.

"I believe we are on an irreversible trend toward more freedom and democracy—but that could change." (Dan Quayle)

"He who fails to plan is planning to fail." (Winston Churchill)

"It ain't over till it's over." (Yogi Berra)

"I can't choose how I feel. But I can choose what I do about it." (Andy Rooney)

"Do not take life too seriously. You'll never get out of it alive." (Elbert Hubbard)

"If you live to be one hundred, you've got it made. Very few people die past that age." (George Burns)

"I was thinking about how people seem to read the Bible a whole lot more as they get older; then it dawned on me — they're cramming for their final exam." (George Carlin

"If you're going to do something tonight that you'll be sorry for tomorrow morning, sleep late." (Henny Youngman)

"Women are wiser than men because they know less and understand more." (James Thurber)

"A failure is like fertilizer; it stinks to be sure, but it makes things grow faster in the future." (Denis Waitley)

"[He] may talk like an idiot, and look like an idiot, but don't let that fool you: he really is an idiot. I implore you, send him back to his father and brothers, who are waiting for him with open arms in the penitentiary. I suggest that we give him ten years in Leavenworth, or eleven years in Twelveworth." (Groucho Marx)

"We made too many wrong mistakes." (Yogi Berra)

"If you find it hard to laugh at yourself, I would be happy to do it for you." (Groucho Marx)

"My wife has to be the worst cook. In my house, we pray after we eat." (Rodney Dangerfield)

I put our scale in the bathroom corner and that's where the little liar will stay until it apologizes.

Few women admit their age. Very few men act theirs.

When I was a kid, I used to watch the Wizard of Oz and wonder how someone could talk if they didn't have a brain. Then I got Facebook.

"Having sex is like playing bridge — if you don't have a good partner, you better have a good hand.: (Andy Rooney)

"I no longer listen to what people say, I just watch what they do. Behavior never lies." (Winston Churchill)

"In the book of life, the answers aren't in the back." (Charles Schulz)

"It's okay to look at the past and the future. Just don't stare." (Lisa Lieberman-Wang)

"Get your facts first, then you can distort them as you please." (Mark Twain)

My IQ test results came back; they were negative.

"Always keep your words soft and sweet, just in case you have to eat them." (Andy Rooney)

"Listen, smile, agree, and then do whatever you were gonna do anyway." (Robert Downey Jr.)

"Wisdom comes from experience. Experience is often a result of lack of wisdom." (Terry Pratchett)

"The reason I talk to myself is because I'm the only one whose answers I accept." (George Carlin)

"Great spirits have always encountered violent opposition from mediocre minds." (Albert Einstein)

"No man goes before his time—unless his boss leaves early." (Groucho Marx)

"When the waitress asked if I wanted my pizza cut into four or eight slices, I said, 'Four. I don't think I can eat eight.'" (Yogi Berra)

"Wine is constant proof that God loves us and loves to see us happy." (Benjamin Franklin)

"As a child my family's menu consisted of two choices: take it or leave it." (Buddy Hackett)

I don't have a beer gut. I have a protective covering for my rock-hard abs.

War does not determine who is right. It determines who is left.

"The secret of a happy marriage remains a secret." (Henny Youngman)

I always take life with a grain of salt. Plus, a slice of lemon. And a shot of tequila.

"I have good looking kids. Thank goodness my wife cheats on me." (Rodney Dangerfield)

"Don't interrupt me while I'm interrupting."
(Winston Churchill)

"Love is the most important thing in the world, but baseball is pretty good, too." (Yogi Berra)

"I'd like to be rich enough so I could throw soap away after the letters are worn off." (Andy Rooney)

"Remember, today is the tomorrow you worried about yesterday." (Dale Carnegie)

"Life doesn't imitate art; it imitates bad television." (Woody Allen)

The surest sign that intelligent life exists elsewhere in the universe is that it has never tried to contact us." (Bill Watterson)

"A day without laughter is a day wasted." (Charlie Chaplin)

"They say marriages are made in Heaven. But so is thunder and lightning." (Clint Eastwood)

"By the time a man realizes that his father was right, he has a son who thinks he's wrong." (Charles Wadsworth)

"Laughing at our mistakes can lengthen our own life. Laughing at someone else's can shorten it." (Cullen Hightower)

I was born to make mistakes, not to fake perfection.

Life is short. Smile while you still have teeth.

"I've learned that opportunities are never lost; someone will take the ones you miss." (Andy Rooney)

Before you speak, make certain you have something worthwhile to say.

"Well, Art is Art, isn't it? Still, on the other hand, water is water. And east is east and west is west, and if you take cranberries and stew them like applesauce they taste much more like prunes than rhubarb does. Now you tell me what you know." (Groucho Marx)

"I wish I had an answer to that because I'm tired of answering that question." (Yogi Berra)

"My sex life is like shooting pool with a rope!" (Rodney Dangerfield)

Life's a soup ...and I'm a fork.

You look like something I drew with my left hand.

"Courage is what it takes to stand up and speak, it's also what it takes to sit down and listen." (Winston Churchill)

The only reason I'm fat is because a tiny body couldn't store all this personality.

"As a kid, I was made to walk the plank. We couldn't afford a dog." (Gary Delaney)

"I saw a documentary on how ships are kept together. Riveting!" (Stewart Francis)

"One thing you'll never hear a Hindu say: 'Ah well... you only live once.'" (Hardeep Singh Kohli)

I'm jealous of my parents, I'll never have a kid as cool as theirs.

"People say I've got no willpower, but I've quit smoking loads of times." (Kai Humphries)

"The greatest lesson in life is to know that even fools are right sometimes." (Winston Churchill)

"My ex-wife is a water sign and I'm an earth sign. Together we made mud." (Rodney Dangerfield)

"I have nothing but respect for you — and not much of that." (Groucho Marx)

"Kindness is the language which the deaf can hear and the blind can see." (Mark Twain)

Just accept the fact that some days you're the pigeon and some days you're the statue.

"The first time I see a jogger smiling, I'll consider it." (Joan Rivers)

"When something is 'new and improved!' which is it? If it's new, then there has never been anything before it. If it's an improvement, then there must have been something before it." (Bill Connolly)

"Let's have some new clichŭs." (Samuel Goldwyn)

"These days, every director bites the hand that laid the golden egg." (Samuel Goldwyn)

"Every man I meet wants to protect me. I can't figure out what from." (Mae West)

Frustration is trying to find your glasses without your glasses.

"If you tell the truth, you don't have to remember anything." (Mark Twain)

"People say that money is not the key to happiness, but I always figured if you have enough money, you can have a key made." (Joan Rivers)

Have you ever tried blindfolded archery? You don't know what you're missing.

My partner's name is David, so we named our son Harley. This way he's Harley, David's son.

"Ladies, I apologize. For all those men who say, 'Why buy the cow when you can get the milk for free?' Here's an update for you: Nowadays 80% of women are against marriage. Why? Because women realize it's not worth buying an entire pig just to get a little sausage!" (Andy Rooney)

"He has all the virtues I dislike and none of the vices I admire." (Winston Churchill)

"It's like dǔja vu all over again." (Yogi Berra)

"My wife is such a bad cook, if we leave dental floss in the kitchen the roaches hang themselves." (Rodney Dangerfield)

"Republicans understand the importance of bondage between parent and child." (Dan Quayle)

Quantity is what you count. Quality is what you count on.

When you're right, no one remembers. When you're wrong, no one forgets.

The road to success is always under construction.

"One word sums up probably the responsibility of any Vice President, and that one word is 'to be prepared.'" (Dan Quayle)

"Go to Heaven for the climate, Hell for the company." (Mark Twain)

"My best birth control now is just to leave the lights on." (Joan Rivers)

"There are a terrible lot of lies going about the world, and the worst of it is that half of them are true." (Winston Churchill)

"The two biggest sellers in any bookstore are the cookbooks and the diet books. The cookbooks tell you how to prepare the food, and the diet books tell you how not to eat any of it." (Andy Rooney)

"You can live to be a hundred if you give up all the things that make you want to live to be a hundred." (Woody Allen)

"I usually take a two-hour nap from 1 to 4." (Yogi Berra)

"Oh, why can't we break away from all this, just you and I, and lodge with my fleas in the hills? I mean flee to my lodge in the hills." (Groucho Marx)

"If beauty is in the eye of the beholder, so is ugliness." (Rodney Dangerfield)

If I wanted to hear the pitter-patter of little feet, I'd put shoes on my cat.

Make yourself at home! Clean my kitchen.

Whatever kind of look you were going for, you missed.

Not all men are annoying. Some are dead.

"One morning I shot an elephant in my pajamas. How he got into my pajamas I'll never know." (Groucho Marx)

"My wife wants sex in the back of the car, and she wants me to drive." (Rodney Dangerfield)

"It gets late early out here." (Yogi Berra)

"I am not part of the problem. I am a Republican." (Dan Quayle)

A clear conscience is usually the sign of a bad memory.

The easiest time to add insult to injury is when you're signing somebody's cast.

You don't need a parachute to go skydiving. You need a parachute to go skydiving *twice*.

Letting go of a loved one can be hard. But sometimes, it's the only way to survive a rock-climbing catastrophe.

"Impotence is nature's way of saying, No hard feelings." (Andy Rooney)

"Education is an admirable thing, but it is well to remember from time to time that nothing that is worth knowing can be taught." (Oscar Wilde)

Q: If you have 3 apples and 4 oranges in one hand and 4 apples and 3 oranges in the other hand, what do you have?
A: Very large hands.

"No man is ever old enough to know better."
(Holbrook Jackson)

A bus station is where a bus stops. A train station is where a train stops. On my desk, I have a workstation.

"I have had a perfectly wonderful evening, but this wasn't it." (Groucho Marx)

"The farther backward you can look, the farther forward you are likely to see." (Winston Churchill)

Time may be a great healer but it's a lousy beautician.

"When I was a boy, the Dead Sea was only sick." (George Burns)

"A man is not old until regrets take the place of dreams." (John Barrymore)

"You're only young once but you can stay immature indefinitely." (Ogden Nash)

There's a veterinarian who prescribes birth-control pills for dogs. It's part of an anti-litter campaign.

I just read that alligators can grow up to 15 feet... but I haven't seen any with more than 4.

Do you think Noah included termites on the ark?

"Nothing in fine print is ever good news." (Andy Rooney)

"The shape I'm in, I could donate my body to science fiction." (Rodney Dangerfield)

Age and treachery will always overcome youth and skill.

"Patriotism is supporting your country all the time, and your government when it deserves it." (Mark Twain)

"How would you like to feel the way she looks? (Groucho Marx)

Alcohol doesn't solve any problem, but neither does milk.

My wallet is like an onion. When I open it, it makes me cry.

"Ninety percent of the game is half mental." (Yogi Berra)

"One night I came home. I figured, let my wife come on. I'll play it cool. Let her make the first move. She went to Florida." (Rodney Dangerfield)

"Success is not final; failure is not fatal: it is the courage to continue that counts. (Winston Churchill)

"We have a firm commitment to Europe. We are a part of Europe." (Dan Quayle)

Q. What do you call a woman who sets fire to all her bills?   A. Bernadette.

I asked a supermarket employee where they kept the canned peaches. He said, 'I'll see,' and he walked away. I asked another and he also said, 'I'll see,' and he, too, walked away. In the end I gave up and found them myself—in Aisle C.

I want to be 14 again and ruin my life differently. I have new ideas.

"The cure for boredom is curiosity. There is no cure for curiosity." (Dorothy Parker)

"To improve is to change; to be perfect is to change often." (Winston Churchill)

"It's hard to be funny when you have to be clean." (Mae West)

"Never answer an anonymous letter." (Yogi Berra)

Did you hear about the guy whose whole left side got amputated? He's alright now.

I was advised to never date a tennis player. Love means nothing to them.

Never date an apostrophe. They can be a little possessive.

At every party, there are two kinds of people: those who want to go home and those who don't.

The trouble is, they're usually married to each other.

"An ounce of prevention is worth a pound of bandages and adhesive tape." (Groucho Marx)

"It's lonely on the top when there's no one on the bottom." (Rodney Dangerfield)

"A drunk was in front of a judge. The judge said, 'You've been brought here for drinking.' The drunk said, 'Okay, let's get started.'" (Henny Youngman)

So what if I can't spell Armageddon! It's not the end of the world.

Sarcasm is the body's natural defense against stupidity.

"If we open a quarrel between the past and the present, we shall find that we have lost the future." (Winston Churchill)

Q: I can only live where there is light, but I die if the light shines on me, what am I?
A: A shadow.

"My psychiatrist told me I was crazy, and I said I want a second opinion. He said, 'Okay, you're ugly too.'" (Rodney Dangerfield)

"I speak two languages: Body and English." (Mae West)

"Marriage is the chief cause of divorce." (Groucho Marx)

Sorry that I'm late. I got here as soon as I wanted to!

"He hits from both sides of the plate. He's amphibious." (Yogi Berra)

It turns out that when asked who your favorite child is, you're supposed to pick out one of your own. I know that now.

It's fine to eat a test grape in the produce section, but you take one bite of rotisserie chicken and it's all, 'Sir, you need to leave!'

"Some people ask the secret of our long marriage. We take time to go to a restaurant two times a week. A little candlelight, dinner, soft music and dancing. She goes Tuesdays, I go Fridays." (Henny Youngman)

"In the course of my life, I have often had to eat my words, and I must confess that I have always found it a wholesome diet." (Winston Churchill)

"You wouldn't have won if we'd beaten you." (Yogi Berra)

"Marry me and I'll never look at another horse!" (Groucho Marx)

"I'm at the age where food has taken the place of sex in my life. In fact, I've just had a mirror put over my kitchen table." (Rodney Dangerfield)

I was going to look for my missing watch, but I couldn't find the time.

I made a graph of my past relationships. It has an ex axis and a why axis.

BREAKING NEWS: Cheese factory explodes in France. Nothing left but de Brie!

"People will generally accept facts as truth only if the facts agree with what they already believe." (Andy Rooney)

"She's been married so many times she has rice marks on her face." (Henny Youngman)

"I wanted to buy a candle holder, but the store didn't have one...so I got a cake." (Mitch Hedberg)

"Instead of past, present and future, I'd prefer chocolate, vanilla, and strawberry." (Ashleigh Brilliant)

"A party without cake is really just a meeting." (Julia Child)

"Ask not what you can do for your country. Ask what's for lunch." (Orson Welles)

"He was a bold man that first ate an oyster." (Jonathan Swift)

"Strength is the capacity to break a chocolate bar into four pieces with your bare hands—and then eat just one of the pieces." (Judith Viorst)

"A doctor gave a man six months to live. The man couldn't pay his bill, so he gave him another six months." (Henny Youngman)

"Age is not a particularly interesting subject. Anyone can get old. All you have to do is live long enough." (Groucho Marx)

"The older we get, the fewer things seem worth waiting in line for." (Will Rogers)

"The third-rate mind is only happy when it's thinking with the majority. The second-rate mind is only happy when it's thinking with the minority. The first-rate mind is only happy when it's thinking." (A.A. Milne)

"Education is not the learning of many facts but the training of the mind to think." (Albert Einstein)

"Before you embark on a journey of revenge, dig two graves." (Confucius)

Those who play by the book will always be beaten by those who write their own.

Little known fact: Before the crowbar was invented, crows simply drank at home.

I may have multiple personalities but none of them like you.

I got a new stick deodorant today. The instructions said: Remove cap and push up bottom.' I can barely walk, but when I fart, the room smells lovely.

"I was married by a judge. I should have asked for a jury." (Groucho Marx)

"I'd be more willing to accept religion, even if I didn't believe it, if I thought it made people nicer to each other, but I don't think it does." (Andy Rooney)

When I finish eating something, I have to show my hands to the dog like I'm a blackjack dealer.

"If you're not a liberal at twenty you have no heart; if you're not a conservative at forty, you have no brain. (Winston Churchill)

"What a doctor I've got—he's really mixed up. Last week, he grabbed my knee and told me to cough. Then he hit me in the balls with a hammer." (Rodney Dangerfield)

I thought the right to bear arms was permission to wear a short-sleeved shirt.

"I stand by all the misstatements that I've made." (Dan Quayle)

"Too caustic? To hell with the cost! We'll make the movie anyway." (Samuel Goldwyn)

"If a little is great, and a lot is better, then way too much is just about right!" (Mae West)

When a man of 60 marries a girl of 21, it's like buying a book for someone else to read.

If you want to lose weight quickly, you could always shave your legs.

Rearrange these letters to form words: 1) PNEIS 2) BUTTSXE Did you get 'SPINE' and 'SUBTEXT'? Yeah...neither did I.

"Man is born free and everywhere he is in chains." (Jean-Jacques Rousseau)

"We've all passed a lot of water since then." (Samuel Goldwyn)

"Society in every state is a blessing but government even in its best state is but a necessary evil; in its worst state an intolerable one." (Thomas Paine)

"Know the rules well, so you can break them effectively." (Dalai Lama)

The only fool bigger than the person who knows it all is the person who argues with him.

"If you don't have wrinkles, you haven't laughed enough." (Phyllis Diller)

"A day without sunshine is like, you know, night." (Steve Martin)

I have to walk early in the morning before my brain figures out what I'm doing.

"What a kid I got, I told him about the birds and the bees, and he told me about the butcher and my wife." (Rodney Dangerfield)

"Always go to other people's funerals; otherwise they won't come to yours." (Yogi Berra)

"I'd like to meet the person who invented sex and see what they're working on now." (Groucho Marx)

"All this criticism… it's like ducks off my back." (Samuel Goldwyn)

"Your birth certificate is an apology letter from the condom factory." (Andy Rooney)

"It ain't the heat, it's the humility." (Yogi Berra)

"Never hold discussions with the monkey when the organ grinder is in the room." (Winston Churchill)

"It is better to die upon your feet than to live upon your knees." (Emiliano Zapata)

"It is the mark of an educated mind to be able to entertain a thought without accepting it." (Aristotle)

"Life is a series of natural and spontaneous changes. Don't resist them; that only creates sorrow. Let reality be reality." (Lao Tzu)

"I'm part of the Jehovah's Witness Protection Program. I get to go door to door and tell people I'm someone else" (Steven Wright)

"To err is human, but it feels divine." (Mae West)

I tried to catch some fog but I mist.

With just a little hard work, you can actually train your cats to do anything they want to do.

Always use a handkerchief. Sneezing into a handkerchief will help your germs collect, so they can grow strong enough to kill you and put you out of your misery.

"My wife only has sex with me for a purpose. Last night it was to time an egg." (Rodney Dangerfield)

"Panties: Not the best thing on earth, but next to the best thing on earth." (Andy Rooney)

"Men occasionally stumble over the truth, but most of them pick themselves up and hurry off as if nothing had happened." (Winston Churchill)

"If you ask me anything I don't know, I'm not going to answer.' (Yogi Berra)

If people are talking behind your back, just fart.

I have loved her from afar for six months now — ever since she got that restraining order.

They say with age comes wisdom, so therefore I don't have wrinkles, I have wise cracks.

"It is one of the blessings of old friends that you can afford to be stupid with them." (Ralph Waldo Emerson)

"The statistics on sanity are that one out of every four Americans is suffering from some form of mental illness. Think of your three best friends. If they're OK, then it's you." (Rita Mae Brown)

"A friend is someone who knows all about you and loves you just the same." (Elbert Hubbard)

"It's the friends you can call up at 4 a.m. that matter." (Marlene Dietrich

Whiteboards are remarkable.

"I made my money the old-fashioned way. I was very nice to a wealthy relative right before he died." (Malcolm Forbes)

"Lots of people want to ride with you in the limo, but what you want is someone who will take the bus with you when the limo breaks down."
(Oprah Winfrey)

"Whoever said money can't buy happiness didn't know where to shop." (Gertrude Stein)

"Money is not the most important thing in the world. Love is. Fortunately, I love money." (Jackie Mason)

Marriage is a three-ring circus: engagement ring, wedding ring, and suffering.

Do unto others before they do unto you.

"We were so poor; in my neighborhood the rainbow was in black—and—white." (Rodney Dangerfield)

"Fear is a reaction. Courage is a decision." (Winston Churchill)

Well, this day was a total waste of makeup.

If I agreed with you, we'd both be wrong.

I love my country. It's the government I'm afraid of!

"A nickel ain't worth a dime anymore." (Yogi Berra)

"The Holocaust was an obscene period in our nation's history. I mean, in this century's history. But we all lived in this century. I didn't live in this century." (Dan Quayle)

"The secret of life is honesty and fair dealing. If you can fake that, you've got it made." (Groucho Marx)

I'd explain it to you but I'm afraid your head might explode.

"If you can make a girl laugh, you can make her do anything." (Marilyn Monroe)

Do you still love nature, despite what it did to

you?

"When I die, I want to die like my grandfather who died peacefully in his sleep. Not screaming like all the passengers in his car." (Will Rogers)

"As you get older three things happen. The first is your memory goes, and I can't remember the other two." (Norman Wisdom)

"Look out for number one and try not to step in number two." (Rodney Dangerfield)

"What is adequacy? Adequacy is no standard at all." (Winston Churchill)

"A woman in love can't be reasonable—or she probably wouldn't be in love." (Mae West)

Some people hear voices... Some see invisible people... Others have no imagination whatsoever.

We have found that it's much easier to restrain our wrath when the other fellow is bigger than we are.

"The most important thing in acting is honesty. Once you've learned to fake that, you're in." (Samuel Goldwyn)

I told my wife I wanted to be cremated. She made me an appointment for Tuesday.

The older I get, the more I understand why roosters just scream to start their day.

"She got her looks from her father. He's a plastic surgeon." (Groucho Marx)

And the Lord said unto John, "Come forth and you will receive eternal life." But John came fifth and won a toaster.

My wife accused me of being immature. I told her to get out of my fort.

"There is nothing government can give you that it hasn't taken from you in the first place." (Winston Churchill"

"I don't know (if they were men or women fans running naked across the field). They had bags over their heads." (Yogi Berra)

"Don't let your opinions sway your judgment." (Samuel Goldwyn)

"The only way to keep your health is to eat what you don't want, drink what you don't like, and do what you'd rather not." (Mark Twain)

If there was a pill to cure procrastination, I would probably take it tomorrow.

I don't hate you, but I'd unplug your life support to charge my phone.

The older I get, the earlier it gets late.

"Age is an issue of mind over matter. If you don't mind, it doesn't matter." (Mark Twain

"Alimony is like buying hay for a dead horse." (Groucho Marx)

"Why buy good luggage? You only use it when you travel." (Yogi Berra)

"I drink too much. The last time I gave a urine sample it had an olive in it." (Rodney Dangerfield)

Seeing how some people wear their masks, I now understand how contraceptives fail.

(Me in heaven): God: 'You're about to get your wings.'
Me: 'Garlic, parmesan or honey barbecue?'
God: 'Get out!'

"I told my psychiatrist that everyone hates me. He said I was being ridiculous — everyone hasn't met me yet." (Rodney Dangerfield)

I'm terrified of elevators so I'm going to start taking steps to avoid them.

The problem with doing nothing is that you don't know when you've finished.

If clothes make the man, you need a makeover.

Not my circus, not my clowns.

I got in touch with my inner self today. That's the last time I'll buy one ply toilet paper at the dollar store.

"Appeasement is feeding the crocodile, hoping he will eat you last." (Winston Churchill)

As I get older and remember all the people I've lost along the way, I think to myself, 'Maybe a career as a tour guide wasn't the right one for me.'

"My mom took me to a dog show, and I won" (Rodney Dangerfield)

"Patience is the art of finding something else to do." (Groucho Marx)

"A doctor said to a man, 'You want to improve your love life? You need to get some exercise. Run ten miles a day. Two weeks later, the man called the doctor, and the doctor asked, 'How is your love life since you have been running?' 'I don't know,' said the man, 'I'm 140 miles away!'" (Henny Youngman)

"We're going to have the best-educated American people in the world." (Dan Quayle)

The main reason Santa is so jolly is because he knows where all the bad girls live.

Did you know that dolphins are so smart that within a few weeks of captivity, they can train people to stand on the very edge of the pool and throw them fish?

God must love stupid people. He made SO many.

"We shape our dwellings, and afterwards our dwellings shape us." (Winston Churchill)

"It was impossible to get a conversation going; everybody was talking too much." (Yogi Berra)

Fighting for peace is like fucking for virginity.

I didn't say it was your fault. I said I was blaming you.

"Quote me as saying I was mis-quoted." (Groucho Marx)

"Most women are attracted to the simple things in life. Like men." (Henny Youngman)

"We sleep in separate rooms. We have dinner apart. We take separate vacations. We're doing everything we can to keep our marriage together." (Rodney Dangerfield)

Struggling to get your wife's attention? Just sit down and look comfortable.

Where did Noah keep his bees? In the ark hives.

Just sold my homing pigeon on eBay for the 22nd time.

"There are only two things you can start without a plan: a riot and a family. For everything else you need a plan." (Groucho Marx)

"Take it with a grin of salt." (Yogi Berra)

"I do not want people to be very agreeable, as it saves me the trouble of liking them a great deal." (Jane Austen)

"Nothing is more dangerous than a friend without discretion; even a prudent enemy is preferable." (Jean de La Fontaine)

"People who think they know everything are a great annoyance to those of us who do." (Isaac Asimov)

"The towels were so thick there I could hardly close my suitcase." (Yogi Berra)

"To build may have to be the slow and laborious task of years. To destroy can be the thoughtless act of a single day." (Winston Churchill)

"Last year my birthday cake looked like a prairie fire." (Rodney Dangerfield)

Now that I've lived during a plague, I understand why most Renaissance paintings are of chubby women lying around without a bra.

I am as swift as a gazelle. An old one. With arthritis. Run over by a Land Rover 8 days ago.

There's a store on Main Street where you can get dead batteries free of charge.

"My brother was a lifeguard in a car wash." (Henny Youngman)

"Illegitimacy is something we should talk about in terms of not having it." (Dan Quayle)

Whatever you may look like, marry a man your own age. As your beauty fades, so will his eyesight.

"If nobody wants to come out to the ballpark, there's nothing you can do to stop them." (Yogi Berra)

I like to spend every day as if it's my last — staying in bed and calling for a nurse to bring me more pudding.

"I cannot say that I don't disagree with you." (Groucho Marx)

"My wife and I have Olympic sex—once every four years." (Rodney Dangerfield)

We cannot start over, but we can begin now, and make a new ending.

Calories are the little bastards that get together at night in your closet and sew your clothes tighter. My closet is infested with the little shits!

Have you ever tried eating a clock? It's very time consuming… especially if you go back for seconds.

"Little League baseball is a very good thing because it keeps the parents off the streets.: (Yogi Berra)

"I told the doctor I broke my leg in two places. He told me to stop going to those places." (Henny Youngman)

"Where do people in hell tell people to go?" (Red Skelton)

Two Wi-Fi engineers got married; the reception was fantastic.

The man who invented Velcro has died. RIP.

The rotation of Earth really makes my day.

"Even Napoleon had his Watergate." (Yogi Berra)

I can tell when people are being judgmental just by looking at them.

"Virginity is not dignity; it's lack of opportunity." (Andy Rooney)

"Socialism is a philosophy of failure, the creed of ignorance, and the gospel of envy; its inherent virtue is the equal sharing of misery." (Winston Churchill)

It takes a lot of balls to golf the way I do.

"I'm not saying my wife is a bad cook but even I know you don't open a grapefruit with a can opener." (Red Skelton)

"Before I speak, I have something important to say." (Groucho Marx)

If you were dating an FBI agent and you broke up, he would be your Fed ex.

My wife first agreed to a date after I gave her a bottle of tonic water. I Schwepped her off her feet.

Be yourself. Everyone else is taken.

"When I was born, I was so surprised I didn't talk for a year and a half." (Gracie Allen)

"Any fool can criticize, condemn, and complain ... and most fools do." (Benjamin Franklin)

"My wife's cooking did a good job of breaking our dog's habit of begging at the table." (Red Skelton)

"With me, nothing goes right. My psychiatrist said my wife and I should have sex every night. Now, we'll never see each other!" (Rodney Dangerfield)

One thing no one ever talks about, when it comes to being an older adult, is how much time we devote to keeping a cardboard box because, you know, it's a really good box.

I can't believe I forgot to go to the gym today. That's seven years in a row, now!

"Pie a la mode… with ice cream." (Yogi Berra)

"Die, my dear? Why, that's the last thing I'll do!" (Groucho Marx)

"Death is a distant rumor to the young." (Andy Rooney)

"My mother always used to say: 'The older you get, the better you get, unless you're a banana.'" (Betty White as Rose on *The Golden Girls*)

"If at first you don't succeed, try, try again. Then quit. There's no point in being a damn fool about it." (W.C. Fields)

Honesty is the best policy, but insanity is a better defense.

I can't talk to you right now… I'm busy sorting M&M's alphabetically.

"The last fight was my fault. My wife asked,
'What's on the TV?'
I said, 'Dust!'" (Red Skelton)

"Blessed are the cracked, for they shall let in the
light." (Groucho Marx)

"I've been in love with the same woman for forty-
one years. If my wife finds out, she'll kill me."
(Henny Youngman)

"I choose a lazy person to do a hard job, because
a lazy person will find an easy way to do it." (Bill
Gates)

"The western part of Pennsylvania is very, uh,
Midwestern. Midwestern. And the eastern part is
more . . . east. Uh, the Midwest . . . Uh,
Pennsylvania is a very important state, a big state.
The western part is—Pennsylvania is a divided
state, like Tennessee is divided into three parts.
Pennsylvania is divided into two parts. You have
western Pennsylvania and then you have eastern
Pennsylvania." (Dan Quayle)

"Never put off till tomorrow what you can do the
day after tomorrow just as well." (Mark Twain)

"Most people work just hard enough not to get
fired and get paid just enough money not to quit."
(George Carlin)

Winter: the season when we try to keep the house as hot as it was in the summer, when we complained about the heat.

Some cause happiness wherever they go, others whenever they go.

I put my grandma on speed dial the other day. I call it insta-gram.

Q: Why did the parents not like their son's biology teacher?
A: He had skeletons in his closet.

"We always hold hands. If I let go, she shops."
(Red Skelton)

"The positive thinker sees the invisible, feels the intangible, and achieves the impossible "
(Winston Churchill)

Q: How does the man in the moon get his hair cut? A: Eclipse it.

Did you hear about the claustrophobic astronaut? He just wanted a little more space.

Q: What do you call a steak that's been knighted by the queen?
A: Sir Loin.

"I refuse to join any club that would have me as a member." (Groucho Marx)

"I'm not going to buy my kids an encyclopedia. Let them walk to school like I did." (Yogi Berra)

"I went to a fight the other night, and a hockey game broke out." (Rodney Dangerfield)

Women should not have children after 35. Really! 35 children are enough!

You are such a good friend that, if we were on a sinking ship together and there was only one life jacket, I'd miss you so much and talk about you fondly to everybody who asked.

A new restaurant opened downtown. It's called 'Karma.' They don't have a menu. You just get what you deserve.

The Pentagon was originally going to be a square, but the contractor kept cutting corners.

What happens if the average number of bullies at a school goes up? The mean increases.

"She has an electric blender, an electric toaster, and an electric bread maker. She said, 'There are too many gadgets and no place to sit down!' So I bought her an electric chair." (Red Skelton)

"If you're going through hell, keep going." (Winston Churchill)

"We have deep depth." (Yogi Berra)

"Age is nothing but experience, and some of us are more experienced than others." (Andy Rooney)

Some people say, 'If you can't beat them, join them'. I say, 'If you can't beat them, beat them', because they will be expecting you to join them, so you will have the element of surprise.

Never hit a man with glasses. Hit him with a baseball bat.

We have enough gun control. What we need is idiot control.

I've met some pricks in my time but you're the full cactus.

"I used to be Snow White, but I drifted." (Mae West)

"This music won't do. There's not enough sarcasm in it." (Samuel Goldwyn)

It's not the fall that kills you; it's the sudden stop at the end.

"Verbosity leads to unclear, inarticulate things." (Dan Quayle)

"I asked my wife where she wanted to go for our anniversary. 'Somewhere I haven't been in a long time,' she said. So I suggested the kitchen." (Red Skelton)

"A girl phoned me the other day and said, 'Come on over. There's nobody home.' So I went over... and nobody was home." (Rodney Dangerfield)

"I married your mother because I wanted children. Imagine my disappointment when you came along." (Groucho Marx)

When I offer to wash your back in the shower, all you have to say is 'yes' or 'no'. Not all this, 'Who are you and how did you get in here?' nonsense.

Why does someone believe you when you say there are four billion stars but check when you say the paint is wet?

"We were overwhelming underdogs." (Yogi Berra)

What's the difference between a northern fairytale and a southern fairytale? A northern fairytale begins 'Once upon a time...'A southern fairytale begins 'Y'all ain't gonna believe this...'

A recent study has found that women who carry a little extra weight live longer than the men who mention it.

I discovered I scream the same way whether I'm about to be devoured by a great white shark or if a piece of seaweed touches my foot.

"Democrats believe people are basically good but must be saved from themselves by their government. Republicans believe people are basically bad, but they'll be okay if they're left alone." (Andy Rooney)

"I saw a piss ant the other day and started thinking, 'Do you step on a piss ant or piss on a step ant?'" (Red Skelton)

"Everyone is in favor of free speech. Hardly a day passes without its being extolled, but some people's idea of it is that they are free to say what they like, but if anyone else says anything back, that is an outrage." (Winston Churchill)

Last night my girlfriend was complaining that I never listen to her... or something like that.

Advice to husbands: Try praising your wife now and then, even if it does startle her at first.

"A hospital bed is a parked taxi with the meter running." (Groucho Marx)

"It's paradoxical that the idea of living a long life appeals to everyone, but the idea of getting old doesn't appeal to anyone." (Andy Rooney)

Always remember you're unique... just like everyone else.

I'm not clumsy — the floor just hates me; the table and chairs are bullies, and the walls get in my way.

I'm not lazy; I'm just very relaxed.

"If you've heard this story before, don't stop me, because I'd like to hear it again." (Groucho Marx)

"My sex life is terrible; my wife put a mirror over our bed. She says she likes to watch herself laugh." (Rodney Dangerfield)

The man who survived both mustard gas and pepper spray is a seasoned veteran now.

Q: Why didn't Han Solo enjoy his steak dinner?
A: It was Chewie.

"My wife told me the car wasn't running well because there was water in the carburetor. I asked where the car was. She told me, 'In the lake.'"
(Red Skelton)

"There are three stages in a man's life — Tri-Weekly, Try Weekly and Try Weakly." (Andy Rooney)

"A nation that forgets its past has no future."
(Winston Churchill)

That is the ugliest top I've ever seen, yet it compliments your face perfectly.

Getting older is just one body part after another saying, 'Ha ha, you think that's bad? Watch this!'

I made a huge 'To Do' list for today. I just can't figure out who's going to do it.

"Personally, I'm always ready to learn, although I do not always like being taught." (Winston Churchill)

"I married Miss Right. I just didn't know her first name was 'Always'." (Red Skelton)

"I never blame myself when I'm not hitting. I just blame the bat, and if it keeps up, I change bats. After all, if I know it isn't my fault that I'm not hitting, how can I get mad at myself?" (Yogi Berra)

"Those are my principles, and if you don't like them... well, I have others." (Groucho Marx)

I spent a lot of time, money and effort childproofing my house... but the kids still get in.

My mother was so surprised when I told her I was born again. She said she didn't feel a thing!

"With girls I get no respect. A belly dancer told me I turned her stomach." (Rodney Dangerfield)

A man comes home and finds his wife with his friend in bed. He shoots his friend dead, and his wife says, 'If you continue to behave like this, you will lose ALL your friends!'

Being a little older, I am very fortunate to have someone call and check on me every day. He is from India and is very concerned about my car warranty.

I choked on a carrot this morning, and all I could think of was, 'I'll bet a doughnut wouldn't have done this to me.'

"Nothing spoils a good story more than the arrival of an eyewitness." (Mark Twain)

Bad puns? That's how eye roll.

My boss is going to fire the employee with the worst posture. I have a hunch it might be me.

I was always taught to respect my elders, but it keeps getting harder to find one.

"My wife's cooking is so bad the flies fix our screens." (Rodney Dangerfield)

"I must confess… I was born at a very early age." (Groucho Marx)

Today, I melted an ice cube with my mind just by staring at it. It took a lot longer than I thought it would.

I grew up with Steve Jobs, Johnny Cash and Bob Hope. Now there are no jobs, no cash, and no hope. Please don't let anything happen to Kevin Bacon.

Think you're old and you will be old. Think you are young, and you will be delusional.

"If I could drop dead right now, I'd be the happiest man." (Samuel Goldwyn)

"When women go wrong, men go right after them." (Mae West)

If you can keep your head when all around you have lost theirs, then you probably haven't understood the seriousness of the situation.

"I think you've got something there, but I'll wait outside until you clean it up." (Groucho Marx)

"When you battle with your conscience and lose, you win." (Henny Youngman)

"Space is almost infinite. As a matter of fact, we think it is infinite." (Dan Quayle)

"I came from a real tough neighborhood. Once a guy pulled a knife on me. I knew he wasn't a professional — the knife had butter on it."
(Rodney Dangerfield)

I run like a girl. Try to keep up.

I'm just working here till a good fast food job opens up.

Don't follow in my footsteps; I walk into walls.

I said no to drugs, but they just wouldn't listen.

"In two words: im possible." (Samuel Goldwyn)

A recent study found that the average golfer walks about 900 miles a year. Another study found that golfers drink, on average, 22 gallons of alcohol a year. That means, on average, golfers get about 41 miles to the gallon. Kind of makes you proud. I almost feel like a hybrid.

Bees don't waste their time explaining to flies that honey is better than shit.

The older I get, the better I was.

"I'm single because I was born that way." (Mae West)

I'm an individual — just like everyone else!

Plumbing company motto: We repair what your husband fixed.

Sign on a travel agency: Go away!

A synonym is a word you use if you can't spell the other one.

"In the school I went to, they asked a kid to prove the law of gravity and he threw the teacher out of the window." (Rodney Dangerfield)

"It's impossible to design anything that is foolproof because fools are so ingenious." (Groucho Marx)

"She ran after the garbage truck, yelling, 'Am I too late for the garbage?' The driver said, 'No, jump in!' (Red Skelton)

This girl said she recognized me from the vegetarian club, but I'd never met herbivore.

Not the brightest crayon in the box now, are we?

I started out with nothing and still have most of it left.

I'm not a complete idiot; some parts are missing.

Everyone thinks I'm psychotic, except for my friends deep inside the earth.

Marriage is when a man and woman become as one; the trouble starts when they try to decide which one.

I'd give my right arm to be ambidextrous.

The best way to get back on your feet is to miss two car payments.

"Military justice is to justice what military music is to music." (Groucho Marx)

"On Halloween, the parents send their kids out looking like me." (Rodney Dangerfield)

I love bacon. Sometimes I eat it twice a day. It takes my mind off the terrible chest pains I keep getting.

"Kites rise highest against the wind, not with it." (Winston Churchill)

As I watch this generation try to rewrite history, one thing I am sure of is that it will be misspelled and have no punctuation.

Driver: What am I supposed to do with this speeding ticket? Officer: Keep it. When you collect four of them, you get a bicycle.

"'Junior, are you pulling the cat's tail?' Junior: 'No, I'm holding on to it ... he's doing the pulling.'" (Red Skelton)

I told my physical therapist that I broke my arm in two places. He told me to stop going to those places.

"Life is full of temporary situations, ultimately ending in a permanent solution." (Rodney Dangerfield)

"The two most important days in your life are the day you were born and the day you find out why." (Mark Twain)

"When you reach the end of your rope, tie a knot in it and hang on." (Franklin D Roosevelt)

"The grass is greener where you water it." (Neil Barringham)

"We do not have to visit a madhouse to find disordered minds; our planet is the mental institution of the universe." (Johann Wolfgang von Goethe)

"An American monkey, after getting drunk on brandy, would never touch it again, and thus is much wiser than most men." (Charles Darwin)

I dialed a number and got the following recording: 'I am not available right now but thank you for caring enough to call. I am making some changes in my life. Please leave a message after the beep. If I don't return your call, you are one of the changes.'

Alcohol! Because no great story started with someone eating a salad.

I don't need a hair stylist. My pillow gives me a new hairstyle every morning.

Don't worry if plan A fails, there are 25 more letters in the alphabet.

Those who play by the book will always be beaten by those who write their own.

If you can't see the bright side of life, polish the dull side.

"You know you're getting old when you stoop to tie your shoelaces and wonder what else you could do while you're down there." (George Burns)

"Eventually, you will reach a point when you stop lying about your age and start bragging about it." (Will Rogers)

"History will have to record that the greatest tragedy of this period of social transition was not the strident clamor of the bad people but the appalling silence of the good people." (Martin Luther King Jr.)

"People know *what* they do; frequently, they know *why* they do what they do, but what they don't know is what they do does." (Michel Foucault)

"Do not condemn the judgment of another because it differs from your own. You may both be wrong." (Dandemis)

"Whatever is my right as a man is also the right of another; and it becomes my duty to guarantee as well as to possess." (Thomas Paine)

"Two times a week we go to a nice restaurant, have a little beverage, good food and companionship. She goes on Tuesdays; I go on Fridays…. We also sleep in separate beds. Hers is in California and mine is in Texas." (Red Skelton)

A dyslexic man walks into a bar….

"Save a boyfriend for a rainy day—and another in case it doesn't rain." (Mae West)

Class trip to the Coca-Cola factory. I hope there's no pop quiz.

PMS jokes aren't funny. Period!

Why were the Indians here first? They had reservations.

Energizer Bunny arrested: charged with battery.

"Remember—Marriage is the number one cause of divorce." (Red Skelton)

When my wife told me to stop impersonating a flamingo, I had to put my foot down.

I'm not saying your perfume is too strong. I'm just saying the canary was alive before you got here.

The teddy bear had to say no to dessert. He was already stuffed.

"My wife's jealousy is getting ridiculous. The other day she looked at my calendar and wanted to know who 'May' was." (Rodney Dangerfield)

(Asked about the message of one of his films) "I'm not interested in messages. Messages are for Western Union." (Samuel Goldwyn

"Ten men waiting for me at the door? Send one of them home, I'm tired." (Mae West)

If you can't live without me, why aren't you dead yet?

Don't tell me the sky is the limit when there are footprints on the moon.

"All discarded lovers should be given a second chance, but with somebody else." (Mae West)

You can't have everything, where would you put it?

Money can't buy happiness, but it sure makes misery easier to live with.

Don't you wish they made a clap on clap off device for some people's mouths?

Of course I talk to myself. Sometimes I need expert advice.

I threw out my back sleeping and tweaked my neck sneezing, so I'm probably just one strong fart away from complete paralysis.

Courage is knowing that something might hurt and doing it anyway. Stupidity is the same thing. That's why life is so hard.

Gravity jokes are getting old, but I fall for them every time.

Do people who climb the world's highest mountain ever rest?

"A fellow told me he was going to hang-glider school. He said, 'I've been going for three months.' I said, 'How many successful jumps do you need to make before you graduate?' He said, 'All of them.'" (Red Skelton)

"Being kind is more important than being right." (Andy Rooney)

"If I wake up in the morning and don't see candles burning and smell flowers, I know it's going to be a good day." (Red Skelton)

"Just give me a comfortable couch, a dog, a good book, and a woman. Then if you can get the dog to go somewhere and read the book, I might have a little fun." (Groucho Marx)

Two fish are sitting in a tank. One looks over at the other and says, 'Hey, do you know how to drive this thing?'

Letting the cat out of the bag is a whole lot easier than putting it back in.

I get enough exercise pushing my luck.

Q: Why do cows have hooves instead of feet?
A: Because they lactose.

"My brother thinks he's a chicken. We don't talk him out of it because we need the eggs."
(Groucho Marx)

"I remember the time I was kidnapped, and they sent a piece of my finger to my father. He said he wanted more proof." (Rodney Dangerfield)

Birthdays are good for you. Statistics show that people who have the most live the longest.

I tried to make a belt out of watches, but it was a waist of time.

My friend asked, 'Why don't cats play poker in the jungle anymore?' I told him it was because there were too many cheetahs.

Life is like a bird. It's pretty cute until it poops on your head.

I threw a ball for my dog. Sure, it was a bit extravagant I know, but it was his birthday, and he looks great in a dinner jacket.

It's never a good idea to keep both feet firmly on the ground. You'll have trouble putting on your pants.

"Courage is rightly esteemed the first of human qualities because it has been said, it is the quality which guarantees all others." (Winston Churchill)

"Bill Dickey is learning me his experience." (Yogi Berra)

I did a theatrical performance on puns. It was a play on words.

"I take my wife everywhere, but she keeps finding her way back." (Red Skelton)

God created the world. Everything else is made in China.

"My friend asked me, 'Red, do you exercise?' I said: 'No, I get plenty of exercise being a pallbearer for my friends that exercised.'" (Red Skelton)

"When I was born, I was so ugly the doctor slapped my mother." (Rodney Dangerfield)

I have one speed, and this is it.

We all get heavier as we get older, because there's a lot more information in our heads. That's my story and I'm sticking to it.

"Television is where you watch people in your living room that you would not want near your house." (Groucho Marx)

Every time I start thinking too much about how I look, I just find a Happy Hour and by the time I leave, I look just fine.

"When I was a kid, I got no respect. I played hide-and-seek. They wouldn't even look for me." (Rodney Dangerfield)

I finally realize why I look so bad in pictures. It's my face.

"I want a movie that starts with an earthquake and works up to a climax." (Samuel Goldwyn)

Do I look like a frigging people person?

You should be glad your diamond is not a carat. That would be an awful price to pay for a vegetable.

Hold on…let me overthink this.

If love is blind, why is lingerie so popular?

Exercise can help you save money. Today I walked home behind the bus and saved $2.00; tomorrow I'm gonna jog home behind a taxi and save $10.00.

Politicians and diapers have one thing in common. They should both be changed regularly, and for the same reason.

I was sitting in traffic the other day… which is probably why I got run over.

"I'm willing to admit that I may not always be right… but I'm never wrong." (Samuel Goldwyn)

"Either he's dead or my watch has stopped." (Groucho Marx)

Q: Why can't you hear a pterodactyl urinate?
A: Because the pee is silent.

Cosmetic surgery used to be such a taboo subject. Now you can talk about Botox, and nobody raises an eyebrow.

My mother never realized the irony in calling me a 'son-of-a-bitch.'

Sex is not the answer. Sex is the question. "Yes" is the answer.

I thought I wanted a career, turns out I just wanted paychecks.

I should've known it wasn't going to work out between my ex-wife and me. After all, I'm a Libra and she's a bitch.

Children: You spend the first two years of their life teaching them how to walk and talk. Then you spend the next sixteen telling them to sit down and shut up.

He who smiles in a crisis has found someone to blame.

"You know you're getting old when you get that one candle on the cake. It's like, 'See if you can blow this out.'" (Jerry Seinfeld)

"True terror is to wake up one morning and discover that your high school class is running the country." (Kurt Vonnegut)

With great reflexes comes great response—ability.

"There is no pleasure worth forgoing just for an extra three years in the geriatric ward." (John Mortimer)

If I'd known I was going to live this long, I'd have taken better care of myself.

How is it one careless match can start a forest fire, but it takes a whole box to start a campfire?

I didn't fight my way to the top of the food chain to be a vegetarian.

She was drop dead gorgeous... like my wife... but in a different way.

If I agreed with you, we'd both be wrong.

"Continuous effort — not strength or intelligence — is the key to unlocking our potential." (Winston Churchill)

"I've never been lucky. The day my ship came in, I was at the airport." (Rodney Dangerfield)

(On the occasion of Yogi Berra Night at Yankee Stadium) "I'm a lucky guy and I'm happy to be with the Yankees. And I want to thank everyone for making this night necessary." (Yogi Berra)

"All men make mistakes, but married men find out about them sooner." (Red Skelton)

We're a non-profit company. It didn't start out that way, but it happened.

"So, I'm ugly. I never saw anyone hit with his face." (Yogi Berra)

"My wife is always trying to get rid of me. The other day she told me to put the garbage out. I said to her I already did. She told me to go and keep an eye on it." (Rodney Dangerfield"

"Yes, darling, let me cover your face with kisses. On second thought, just let me cover your face." (Groucho Marx)

"I haven't spoken to my wife in 18 months. I don't like to interrupt her." (Red Skelton)

Old age is when broadness of the mind and narrowness of the waist change places.

I'm busy now. Can I ignore you some other time?

"Attitude is a little thing that makes a big difference." (Winston Churchill)

A TV can insult your intelligence, but nothing rubs it in like a computer.

Muffler Shop Motto: No appointment necessary. We hear you coming.

People who complain about taxes can be divided into two classes: men and women.

I just want revenge. Is that so wrong?

"Virginity can be cured." (Andy Rooney)

"I told my dentist my teeth are going yellow. He told me to wear a brown tie." (Rodney Dangerfield)

"How can you think and hit at the same time?" (Yogi Berra)

"She got a mud pack and looked great for two days. Then the mud fell off." (Red Skelton)

(On *You Bet Your Life*, after learning that a young-looking female contestant had nine children.) "I love my cigar, but I take it out once in a while." (Groucho Marx)

This is our new and improved system. It just doesn't work as well as the old one.

I believe you ...but thousands wouldn't.

I used to be conceited, but now I'm perfect.

My wife says I never listen to her (or something like that).

I joined a health club last year, spent about 400 bucks. Haven't lost a pound. Apparently, you have to go there.

Every time I hear the dirty word 'exercise,' I wash my mouth out with chocolate.

The advantage of exercising every day is so when you die, they'll say, 'Well, she looks good doesn't she?'

If you are going to try cross-country skiing, start with a small country.

"Why do they have a handicapped parking spot in front of a liquor store?" (Red Skelton)

"Who are you going to believe—me or your own eyes?" (Groucho Marx)

"Everyone wants to live on top of the mountain, but all the happiness and growth occurs while you're climbing it." (Andy Rooney)

I used to jog 5 miles a day... then I found a short cut.

"I told my wife the truth. I told her I was seeing a psychiatrist. Then she told me the truth: that she was seeing a psychiatrist, two plumbers, and a bartender." (Rodney Dangerfield)

Authority is granted. Respect is earned.

"Let's bring it up to date with some snappy nineteenth century dialogue." (Samuel Goldwyn)

Apart from being physically exhausted, financially challenged, overweight and mentally unstable, everything's going really well. Thanks.

Ask your doctor if a drug with 32 pages of side effects is bad for you.

I relabeled all of the jars in my wife's spice rack. I'm not in trouble yet, but the thyme is cumin.

I just read a book about marriage that says to treat your wife like you treated her on your first date.

So tonight, after dinner, I'm dropping her off at her parent's house.

"My golf game is getting really good. Last week, I got through the windmill." (Rodney Dangerfield)

"I find television very educating. Every time somebody turns on the set, I go into the other room and read a book." (Groucho Marx)

Do you ever get up in the morning, look in the mirror and think, 'That can't be accurate!'

I'd love to help you, but I don't even play an active role in my own life anymore.

If your phone doesn't ring, it'll be me.

Never give up on your dreams. Stay in bed and sleep on.

"Old age isn't so bad if you consider the alternative." (Maurice Chevalier)

"Right is right, even if everyone is against it; and wrong is wrong, even if everyone is for it." (William Penn)

You know you're getting old when everything hurts, and what doesn't hurt doesn't work.

"Never was anything great achieved without danger." (Niccolò Machiavelli)

When chemists die, they barium.

Don't stress about your eyesight failing as you get older. It's nature's way of protecting you from shock as you walk past the mirror.

"My father carries around the picture of the kid who came with his wallet." (Rodney Dangerfield)

Don't take criticism from anyone from whom you would never seek advice.

"Every accomplishment starts with the decision to try." (John F. Kennedy)

Don't depend too much on anyone in this world. Even your shadow leaves you when you're in darkness.

"I'm not a vegetarian, but I eat animals who are." (Groucho Marx)

I know I got a lot of exercise the last few years...... just getting over the hill.

"When you're 20 you care what everyone thinks, when you're 40 you stop caring what everyone thinks, when you're 60 you realize no one was ever thinking about you in the first place. You have enemies? Good. That means you've stood up for something, sometime in your life." (Winston Churchill)

It only takes one slow—walking person in the grocery store to destroy the illusion that I'm a nice person.

"With my dog I don't get no respect. He keeps barking at the front door. He doesn't want to go out. He wants me to leave." (Rodney Dangerfield)

If you're not supposed to eat at night, why is there a light bulb in the refrigerator?

Don't drink while driving – you might spill some.

I refuse to answer that question on the grounds that I don't know the answer.

Doesn't expecting the unexpected make the unexpected expected?

I asked God for a bike, but I know God doesn't work that way. So I stole a bike and asked for forgiveness.

You're born free, then you're taxed to death.

I am nobody. Nobody is perfect. I am perfect.

"Be open minded, but not so open minded that your brains fall out." (Groucho Marx)

"The price of greatness is responsibility.:"
(Winston Churchill)

"I walked in on my wife and the milkman, the first thing she says is Don't tell the butcher." (Rodney Dangerfield)

True friendship isn't about being inseparable; it's about being separated and nothing changes.

A fake friend can cause much more damage than a real enemy.

"Some have been thought brave because they were afraid to run away." (Henny Youngman)

"Hawaii is a small state. It is a state that is by itself. It is a—it is different than the other forty-nine states. Well, all states are different, but it's got a particularly unique situation.... Hawaii has always been a very pivotal role in the Pacific. It is in the Pacific. It is a part of the United States that is an island that is right here." (Dan Quayle)

"At age 20, we worry about what others think of us. At age 40, we don't care what they think of us. At age 60, we discover they haven't been thinking of us at all." (Ann Landers)

"Age is an issue of mind over matter. If you don't mind, it doesn't matter." (Mark Twain)

Jokes about German sausage are the wurst.

A soldier who survived mustard gas and pepper spray is now a seasoned veteran.

I know a guy who's addicted to brake fluid. He says he can stop at any time.

"My kids scotch tape worms to the sidewalk and watch the birds get hernias." (Rodney Dangerfield)

I wouldn't let my children go to see the orchestra. There's too much sax and violins.

"Some people ask the secret of our long marriage. We take time to go to a restaurant two times a week. A little candlelight, dinner, soft music, and dancing. She goes Tuesdays, I go Fridays." (Henny Youngman)

Did you hear about the thieves who robbed a theatre during a performance? They stole the spotlight.

I'm a perfectionist with a procrastinator complex. Someday I'm going to be awesome.

"Schools have not necessarily much to do with education...they are mainly institutions of control where certain basic habits must be inculcated in the young. Education is quite different and has little place in school." (Winston Churchill)

"Money will not make you happy, and happy will not make you money." (Groucho Marx)

I accidentally swallowed a bunch of Scrabble tiles. My next trip to the bathroom could spell disaster.

No animals were used in testing this product... only stupid humans.

I told my wife I felt like a deck of cards, and she said she'd deal with me later.

I have a weird talent where I can tell what's inside a wrapped present. It's a gift.

Did you hear about the English teacher who went to jail? She got a full sentence.

My math teacher called me average. How mean!

I used to be indecisive. Now I'm not sure.

My therapist says I have a preoccupation with vengeance. We'll see about that.

My first experience with culture shock? Probably when I peed on an electric fence.

"I don't get no respect. I called Suicide Prevention. They tried to talk me into it." (Rodney Dangerfield)

"Mars is essentially in the same orbit. Mars is somewhat the same distance from the Sun, which is very important. We have seen pictures where there are canals, we believe, and water. If there is water, that means there is oxygen. If oxygen, that means we can breathe." (Dan Quayle)

"Women should be obscene, not heard." (Groucho Marx)

"The secret of staying young is to live honestly, eat slowly, and lie about your age." (Lucille Ball)

"Old age is always fifteen years older than I am." (Oliver Wendell Holmes Jr.)

"I am a friend of the working man, and I would rather be his friend than be one." (Clarence Darrow)

"If you think your boss is stupid, remember— you wouldn't have a job if he was any smarter." (John Gotti)

"Anybody who tells you money can't buy happiness never had any." (Samuel L. Jackson)

"Money cannot buy health, but I'd settle for a diamond-studded wheelchair." (Dorothy Parker)

I'm skeptical of anyone who tells me they do yoga every day. That's a bit of a stretch.

There's nothing scarier than that split second when you lose your balance in the shower and you think, 'They're going to find me naked!'

If you think you're smarter than the previous generation... 50 years ago the owner's manual of a car showed you how to adjust the valves. Today, it warns you not to drink the contents of the battery.

I got a seniors' GPS. Not only does it tell me how to get to my destination, it also tells me why I wanted to go there.

I used to work as an origami teacher, but I hated it. There was too much paperwork.

I've been on three dates with a guy who works at a zoo. I think he's a keeper.

I am busy right now; can I ignore you some other time?

I changed my password to 'Incorrect.' Now, when I can't remember my password, my computer says my password is 'incorrect.'

"Last time I saw a mouth like that, it had a hook in it." (Rodney Dangerfield)

I don't have an attitude problem. You have a *perception* problem.

Before you marry a person, you should first make them use a computer with a slow Internet connection to see who they really are.

I used to date a girl who was lactose intolerant, but we had to break up. She couldn't stomach my cheesy jokes.

"I am fond of pigs. Dogs look up to us. Cats look down on us. Pigs treat us as equals." (Winston Churchill)

"I've been looking for a girl like you — not you, but a girl like you." (Groucho Marx)

You'll never guess who I bumped into on the way to the opticians! Everyone.

To whoever stole my broken bathroom scales, you'll never get a weigh with it.

I lift weights only on Saturday and Sunday because Monday to Friday are weak days.

Q: Why are fish the easiest animals to weigh?
A: Because they come with their own scales.

I started a business selling yachts in my attic. Sails have gone through the roof.

"If you are not having fun, you are doing something wrong." (Groucho Marx)

True friendship isn't about being inseparable; it's about being separated and nothing changes.

You know when people say, 'It's always the last place you look.' Of course, it is. Why would you keep looking after you've found it?

If you drop something when you were younger, you just picked it up. When you're older and you drop something, you stare at it for just a bit contemplating if you actually need it anymore.

I like to make lists. I also like to leave them laying on the kitchen counter, and then guess what's on the list when I am at the store.

"It is not enough that we do our best; sometimes we must do what is required." (Winston Churchill)

If you've never seen the Devil face-to-face, you're probably walking in the same direction.

From the moment I saw you I knew I was going to spend the rest of my life avoiding you.

Due to my time alone, I finished three books yesterday. And believe me, that's a lot of coloring.

I encouraged my wife to embrace her mistakes. She gave me a big hug.

If ignorance is bliss, why aren't more people happy?

My patience has stretch marks.

A will is a dead giveaway.

I used to be a banker, but I lost interest.

The shovel was a ground—breaking invention.

"I worked my way up from nothing to a state of extreme poverty." (Groucho Marx)

My wife and I had words, but I didn't get to use mine.

"For myself I am an optimist — it does not seem to be much use to be anything else." (Winston Churchill)

The easiest time to add insult to injury is when you're signing somebody's cast.

Why does someone believe you when you say there are four billion stars but checks when you say the paint is wet?

When tempted to fight fire with fire, always remember that the fire department usually uses water.

Coffee backwards is eeffoc. Until I have my coffee in the morning, I don't give eeffoc.

I enjoy a glass of wine every night for the health benefits. The other glasses are for my witty comebacks and flawless dance moves.

Q: What do you call the wife of a hippie?
A: Mississippi.

"When you're in jail, a good friend will be trying to bail you out. A best friend will be in the cell next to you saying, 'Damn, that was fun.'" (Groucho Marx)

"I told my wife a man is like wine; he gets better with age. She locked me in the cellar." (Rodney Dangerfield)

Trust before you love, know before you judge, commit before you promise, forgive before you forget, and appreciate before you regret.

6:30 is the best time on a clock, hands down.

"Budget: a way of going broke methodically." (Groucho Marx)

You have to be 100% behind someone before you can stab them in the back.

The irony of life is that, by the time you're old enough to know your way around, you're not going anywhere.

A computer once beat me at chess, but it was no match for me at kick boxing.

I saw a woman wearing a sweatshirt with "Guess" on it...so I guessed, 'Implants?'

The shinbone is a device for finding furniture in a dark room.

Good girls are bad girls that never get caught.

Laugh at your problems. Everybody else does.

Crowded elevators smell different to midgets.

Women will never be equal to men until they can walk down the street with a bald head and a beer gut, and still think they are sexy.

"At my age I'm envious of a stiff wind. (Rodney Dangerfield)

"The real question for 1988 is whether we're going to go forward to tomorrow, or past to the . . . to the back." (Dan Quayle)

When I was a child, my father told me I could be anyone I wanted to be. Nowadays, they call that identity theft.

I have a broken barometer that I need to sell. No pressure.

If I'm smiling, I'm contemplating doing something really bad. If I'm laughing, I've already done it.

"The future will be better tomorrow." (Dan Quayle)

"I looked up my family tree and found out I was the sap." (Rodney Dangerfield)

"I've put on a lot of weight... I only weighed six and a half pounds when I was born." (Red Skelton)

"When the eagles are silent, the parrots begin to jabber." (Winston Churchill)

"You tell the stupidest questions." (Yogi Berra)

"Politics is the art of looking for trouble, finding it everywhere, diagnosing it incorrectly and applying the wrong remedies." (Groucho Marx)

You'll always stay young if you live honestly, eat slowly, sleep sufficiently, work industriously, worship faithfully, and lie about your age.

Q: How can you tell you're getting old?
A: When you go to an antique auction and three people bid on you.

Knowledge is power, and power corrupts, so study hard and be evil.

Isn't it odd the way everyone automatically assumes that the goo in soap dispensers is always soap? I like to fill mine with mustard, just to teach people a lesson in trust.

A TV can insult your intelligence. But nothing rubs it in like a computer.

When tempted to fight fire with fire, always remember... The fire department usually uses water.

You are such a good friend that, if we were on a sinking ship together and there was only one life jacket, I'd miss you so much and talk about you fondly to everybody who asked.

Some cause happiness wherever they go. Others *whenever* they go.

It's not the fall that kills you. It's the sudden stop at the end.

Don't trust atoms, they make up everything.

"My wife gives good headache." (Rodney Dangerfield)

"Middle age is when you go to bed at night and hope you feel better in the morning. Old age is when you go to bed at night and hope you wake up in the morning. — Groucho Marx

This isn't a particularly novel observation, but the world is full of people who think they can manipulate the lives of others merely by getting a law passed." (Groucho Marx)

I can't believe I got fired from the calendar factory. All I did was take a day off.

Today a man knocked on my door and asked for a small donation toward the local swimming pool. I gave him a glass of water.

The future, the present, and the past walk into a bar; things got a little tense.

I didn't think orthopedic shoes would help, but I stand corrected.

It was an emotional wedding. Even the cake was in tiers.

Just got fired from my job as a set designer. I left without making a scene.

"Time wounds all heels." (Groucho Marx)

The world champion tongue twister got arrested, I hear they're going to give him a tough sentence.

Refusing to go to the gym is a form of resistance training.

"In America you can go on the air and kid the politicians, and the politicians can go on the air and kid the people." (Groucho Marx)

I used to work in a shoe recycling shop. It was sole destroying.

Why was it so hot in the stadium after the baseball game? All the fans left!

I'm not sure if my ceiling is the best in the world, but it's definitely up there.

It is said that if you line up all the cars in the world end to end, someone would be stupid enough to try to pass them.

I could say nice things about you, but I would rather tell the truth.

I like dogs too. Let's exchange recipes.

Forget the Joneses... I can't keep up with the Simpsons.

Few women admit their age; Fewer men act it.

"I intend to live forever or die trying." (Groucho Marx)

"I had plenty of pimples as a kid. One day I fell asleep in the library. When I woke up, a blind man was reading my face." (Rodney Dangerfield)

A balanced diet means a cupcake in each hand.

Doing nothing is hard. You never know when you're done.

Never argue with an idiot. He'll drag you down to his level and beat you with experience.

Stalin should have known communism wouldn't work. There were red flags everywhere.

I own a pencil that used to be owned by William Shakespeare, but he chewed it a lot. Now I can't tell if it's 2B or not 2B.

Someone sent ten different puns to friends, with the hope that at least one of the puns would make them laugh. No pun in ten did.

Q: How does Moses make tea? A: He brews it.

I stayed up all night to see where the sun went, then it dawned on me.

"A dame that knows the ropes isn't likely to get tied up." (Mae West)

Coffee, chocolate, men... some things are just better rich.

"All people are born alike — except Republicans and Democrats." (Groucho Marx)

"I came from a real tough neighborhood. Every time I shut the window, I hurt somebody's fingers." (Rodney Dangerfield)

"When I have been asked during these last weeks who caused the riots and the killing in L.A., my answer has been direct and simple. Who is to blame for the riots? The rioters are to blame. Who is to blame for the killings? The killers are to blame." (Dan Quayle)

My wife just found out I replaced our bed with a trampoline, she hit the ceiling!

The last thing I want to do is hurt you; but it's still on the list.

Before you criticize someone, walk a mile in their shoes. That way, when you do criticize them, you're a mile away and you have their shoes.

I never knew what happiness was until I got married—and then it was too late.

A rich man is one who isn't afraid to ask the clerk to show him something cheaper.

The trouble with getting to work on time is that it makes the day so long.

Before you marry a person, you should first make them use a computer with a slow Internet connection to see who they really are.

How do you make holy water? You boil the hell out of it.

I threw a boomerang a couple years ago; now I live in constant fear.

I was addicted to the hokey pokey, but then I turned myself around.

"Military intelligence is a contradiction in terms."
(Groucho Marx)

"Think what a better world it would be if we all,
the whole world, had cookies and milk about
three o'clock every afternoon and then lay down
on our blankets for a nap." (Barbara Jordan)

I have a few jokes about unemployed people, but
none of them work.

Blunt pencils are really pointless.

A fish swam into a concrete wall, Dam!

The guy who got hit in the head with a can of soda
was lucky it was a soft drink.

The man who invented knock-knock jokes should
get a no bell prize.

Why be difficult when, with a little bit of effort,
you can be impossible?

I'd far rather be happy than right.

Lab reports are always my dog's favorite
homework assignment.

The easiest job in the world has to be a coroner.
What's the worst thing that could happen? If
everything goes wrong, maybe you'd get a pulse.

Build a man a fire, and he'll be warm for a day. Set a man on fire, and he'll be warm for the rest of his life.

You'll always stay young if you live honestly, eat slowly, sleep sufficiently, work industriously, worship faithfully, and lie about your age.

"Anyone who says he can see through women is missing a lot." (Groucho Marx)

"I stuck my head out the window and got arrested for mooning." (Rodney Dangerfield)

Things always go according to plan…when you're making it up as you go along.

A bank is a place that will lend you money, if you can prove that you don't need it.

I heard there were a bunch of break-ins over at the car park. That is wrong on so many levels.

Are people born with photographic memories, or does it take time to develop?

My friend's bakery burned down last night. Now his business is toast.

Four fonts walk into a bar. The bartender says, 'Hey! We don't want your type in here!'

A ghost walked into a bar and ordered a shot of vodka. The bartender said, 'Sorry, we don't serve spirits here.'

The kid who started a business tying shoelaces on the playground? It was a knot-for-profit.

When I lose the TV controller, it's always hidden in some remote destination.

If you arrest a mime, do you have to tell him he has the right to remain silent?

"With my wife I get no respect. I fell asleep with a cigarette in my hand, and she lit it." (Rodney Dangerfield)

Allow me to introduce my selves.

I asked my date to meet me at the gym, but she never showed up. I guess we aren't going to work out.

I told my son, if you are intimidated by a date, remember one thing: they are just big raisins.

My friends didn't like their son's biology teacher. He had too many skeletons in his closet.

We have enough youth. How about a Fountain of Smart?

There was a kid who started a business tying shoelaces on the playground. It was a knot-for-profit.

A positive attitude may not solve all your problems. But it will annoy enough people to make it worth the effort.

Q: How do construction workers party?
A: They raise the roof.

An expensive laxative will give you a run for your money.

Nuns wear the same outfit every day. Must be a habit, I guess.

Your lack of planning is not my emergency.

I have one nerve left and you're getting on it.

To err is human. To forgive is unusual.

"I knew a girl so ugly that she was known as a two-bagger. That's when you put a bag over your head in case the bag over her head breaks." (Rodney Dangerfield)

I read recipes the same way I read science fiction. I get to the end and I think, "Well, *that's* not going to happen."

I can't believe I got fired from the calendar factory. All I did was take a day off.

I'm feeling pretty proud of myself. The puzzle I bought said 3-5 years, but I finished it in 18 months.

My first job was working in an orange juice factory, but I got canned: couldn't concentrate.

You shouldn't kiss anyone on Jan. 1 because it's only the first date.

My friend set me up on a blind date and he said, I'd better warn you, she's expecting a baby. I felt like such an idiot sitting in the bar wearing nothing but a diaper.

My girlfriend dated a clown right before she met me. I've got some big shoes to fill.

"What a childhood I had, why, when I took my first step, my old man tripped me!" (Rodney Dangerfield)

I tried sniffing coke once, but the ice cubes stuck in my nose.

It must be hard lugging around that enormous brain of yours.

Sarcasm is just one more service we offer.

How is it one careless match can start a forest fire, but it takes a whole box to start a campfire?

Don't worry. I forgot your name, too!

Why does a slight tax increase cost you $200 and a substantial tax cut save you 30 cents?

I have selective hearing. Sorry, you weren't selected today... and tomorrow isn't looking good either.

Knowledge is knowing a tomato is a fruit. Wisdom is not putting a tomato in a fruit salad.

Money can't buy happiness, but it sure makes misery easier to live with.

How does NASA organize a party? They planet

I used to be addicted to soap but I'm clean now.

I went on a once-in-a-lifetime holiday. Never again.

Exaggerations went up by one million per cent last year.

I've decided to sell my Hoover. It was just collecting dust.

Q: What kind of exercise do lazy people do?
A: Diddly-squats.

Q: Why did the chicken go to the sñance?
A: To get to the other side.

Q: What sits at the bottom of the sea and twitches? A: A nervous wreck.

My friend said to me: 'What rhymes with orange? I said: 'No. it doesn't!'

Q: Did you hear about the claustrophobic astronaut?
A: He needed a little space.

I've found a job helping a one-armed typist do capital letters. It's shift work.

Have you heard about those new corduroy pillows? They're making headlines.

As a scarecrow, people say I'm outstanding in my field. But, hay, it's in my jeans.

What do you call a parade of rabbits hopping backwards? A receding hare-line.

What's the best thing about Switzerland? I don't know, but the flag is a big plus.

Sometimes I tuck my knees into my chest and lean forward. That's just how I roll.

I may not be special, but I am a very limited edition.

Nothing is interesting if you're not interested.

If winning isn't everything, why do we keep score?

Life is like ice cream—to be enjoyed before it melts.

I don't need your attitude. I've got one of my own, thank you.

Research is what I'm doing when I don't know what I'm doing.

My goal this year was to lose 10 pounds. I've just got 13 to go.

Only those who really care about you can hear you when you're quiet.

I thought I'd found the key to success, but someone changed the lock.

If you think I'm sarcastic, it's a good thing you never hear what I don't say.

If you have an opinion about my attitude, raise your hand. Now stick it in your mouth.

Yesterday I did nothing and today, I need to finish what I was doing yesterday.

If a woman says to a man, 'Do what you want…,' the man would be unwise to follow her advice.

If you're caught doing something you shouldn't have been doing, just act daft.

I don't hate you. I'd unplug your life support to recharge my phone, but I don't hate you.

If you're wondering whether I'm free tomorrow, I'll tell you now that I'm likely to be very expensive.

Don't confuse my personality with my attitude. My personality depends on me. My attitude depends on you.

Hear about the new restaurant called 'Karma'? There's no menu; you only get what you deserve.

I saw a guy spill all his Scrabble letters on the road. So I asked him, 'What's the word on the street?'

A man tells his doctor, Help me. I'm addicted to Twitter!' To which the doctor replied, 'Sorry, I'm not following you.'

"Every moment is a fresh beginning." (T.S Eliot)

"You must do the things you think you cannot do." (Eleanor Roosevelt)

Work hard in silence, let your success be the noise.

"Start where you are. Use what you have. Do what you can." (Arthur Ashe)

Never let your best friends get lonely, keep disturbing them.

Sometimes I wish I was an octopus, so I could slap eight people at once.

If Cinderella's shoe fit perfectly, then why did it fall off?

"Life is ours to be spent, not to be saved." (D. H. Lawrence)

Papercut: A tree's final moment of revenge.

Common sense is like deodorant— those who need it the most never use it.

"It's never too late for a new beginning in your life." (Joyce Meyer)

"Life begins at the end of your comfort zone." (Neale Donald Walsch)

"Thoughts lead to feelings. Feelings lead to actions. Actions leads to results." (T. Harv Eker)

If you're hotter than me, that means I'm cooler than you.

My wallet is like an onion. Opening it makes me cry.

My goal this weekend is to move, just enough so people don't think I'm dead.

Lazy people fact #2347827309018287. You were too lazy to read that number.

"Everything you can imagine is real." (Pablo Picasso)

Life always offers you a second chance. It's called tomorrow.

My six pack is protected by a layer of fat.

When nothing is going right, go left.

If you have crazy friends, you have everything you'll ever need.

Find your patience before I lose mine.

Are you always this retarded or are you making a special effort today?

Person 1: 'Watch my stuff.'
Person 2: 'Why? Is it going to do a trick?'

I clapped because it's finished, not because I like it.

That's a pretty dress. Too bad you couldn't find it in your size.

Here let me drop what's important to me and pay attention to you and all of your needs.

Keep rolling your eyes. Maybe you'll find a brain back there.

I believe in annoyed at first sight.

I've reached that age where my brain goes from 'You probably shouldn't say that' to 'What the hell! Let's see what happens.'

Revenge is beneath me. However, accidents will happen.

I don't have the energy to pretend to like you today.

Silence is golden, unless you have kids, then silence is just plain suspicious.

I'm not running away from hard work; I'm too lazy to run.

Don't make me laugh, I'm trying to be mad at you.

If I won the award for laziness, I would send somebody to pick it up for me.

Maybe if we tell people the brain is an app, they'll start using it.

My bed is a magical place where I suddenly remember everything I forgot to do.

"Even the darkest night will end, and the sun will rise." (Victor Hugo)

Why was six scared of seven? Because seven "ate" nine.

I only check my voicemail to get rid of the annoying little icon.

My windows aren't dirty, my dog is painting.

"Happiness is not by chance, but by choice." (Jim Rohn)

"Everything has beauty, but not everyone sees it." (Confucius)

"Why fit in when you were born to stand out." (Dr. Seuss)

"Try to be a rainbow in someone's cloud." (Maya Angelou)

The quieter you become, the more you can hear.

At night, I can't fall asleep. In the morning, I can't get up.

Some people are like clouds. When they go away, it's a brighter day.

"Better to do something imperfectly than to do nothing flawlessly." (Robert H. Schuller)

"Wherever you go, go with all your heart." (Confucius)

A best friend is like a four-leaf clover, hard to find, lucky to have.

Seeing a spider in my room isn't scary. It's scary when it disappears.

If we shouldn't eat at night, why is there a light in the fridge?

They say, 'don't try this at home,' so I'm coming over to your house to try it.

When you fall, I will be there to catch you with love. Sincerely, the floor.

Lottery: a tax on people who are bad at math.

IRS: We've got what it takes to take what you have got.

What happens to a frog's car when it breaks down? It gets toad away.

I didn't fall, I'm just spending some quality time with the floor.

Today, I laughed until my abs started hurting, so I can skip the gym.

"How people treat you is their karma, how you react is yours.) (Wayne Dyer)You have no one to blame but yourself. Unless some other guy is standing next to you then you can blame him.

Person 1: 'OMG did you just fall?'
Person 2: 'No, the ground just came up and smacked me in my face!'
Person 1: 'Do you want a piece of my mind?'
Person 2: 'Oh no, I couldn't take the last piece.'

I thought I had seen the pinnacle of stupid. Then I met you.

Q: 'Do you know who I am?'
A: 'Why? Have you forgotten?'

You always do me a favor when you shut up!

If you press the elevator button three times it goes into hurry mode – really.

(While I'm washing my car) Person: 'Hey what's up? Washing your car?'
Me: 'No, I'm watering it to see if it'll grow into a bus.'

What did I do to give you the impression I actually care about what you think?

If I wanted to kill myself, I would climb your ego and jump to your IQ.

There's no need to repeat yourself. I ignored you just fine the first time.

"Tough times never last, but tough people do." (Robert H. Schuller)

"You have to make the rules, not follow them." (Isaac Newton)

"No one has ever become poor by giving." (Anne Frank)

My level of sarcasm has gotten to the point where I don't even know if I'm kidding or not.

Of course, I am athletic. I surf the Internet every day.

My silence spoke a thousand words, but you never heard them.

I really should do something with my life. Maybe tomorrow.

When the past comes knocking, don't answer. It has nothing new to tell you.

Waiting until the movie starts to eat your popcorn is one of the hardest things in the world.

I love my job only when I'm on vacation.

Always follow your heart but remember to bring your brain along.

It's alright if you don't agree with me; I can't force you to be right.

I solemnly swear that I am up to no good.

"It is never too late to be what you might have been." (George Eliot)

One day or day one? You decide!

About the Editor

A former city and property manager, college professor, and judge, Andrew Felder is a part-time attorney and full-time editor and publisher of The Network Magazine. The author of several books, he has tackled a wide variety of subject matter including humor, psychology, and romance. A native New Yorker, and the father of three and grandfather of seven, he currently lives in Fort Worth with his wife, Bette, and Aussiedoodle, Annabelle.

www.ingramcontent.com/pod-product-compliance
Lightning Source LLC
Chambersburg PA
CBHW010321180726
47991CB00023B/3243